HEAVENLY CROWNS

Also by Heather Whitestone McCallum and Angela Hunt

Let God Surprise You

HEATHER WHITESTONE MCCALLUM
and ANGELA HUNT

HEAVENLY CROWNS

*Striving for
a Godly Life in the
Midst of Daily Struggles*

ZONDERVAN™

GRAND RAPIDS, MICHIGAN 49530 USA

ZONDERVAN™

Heavenly Crowns
Copyright © 2004 by Heather Whitestone McCallum and Angela Elwell Hunt

Requests for information should be addressed to:

Zondervan, *Grand Rapids, Michigan 49530*

Library of Congress Cataloging-in-Publication Data

Whitestone-McCallum, Heather.
    Heavenly crowns: striving for a godly life in the midst of daily struggles /
Heather Whitestone McCallum and Angela Hunt.
      p. cm.
    Includes bibliographical references.
    ISBN 0-310-24627-X
    1. Christian women—Religious life. 2. Crowns—Religious aspects—
Christianity. 3. Whitestone-McCallum, Heather. I. Hunt, Angela Elwell,
1957–II. Title.
BV4527.W49 2004
248.8'43—dc22   2003020237

Published in association with the literary agency of Alive Communications, Inc.,
7680 Goddard Street, Suite 200, Colorado Springs, CO 80920.

Interior design by Michelle Espinoza

Printed in the United States of America

04 05 06 07 08 09 10 /❖ DC/ 10 9 8 7 6 5 4 3 2 1

To every woman who still carries
a little girl's dream of being a princess
And every man who still carries
a little boy's dream of being a hero
Keep your dreams alive in Jesus' name
For your crowns are waiting for you in heaven

We want to hear from you. Please send your comments about this book to us in care of zreview@zondervan.com. Thank you.

ZONDERVAN™

GRAND RAPIDS, MICHIGAN 49530 USA

WWW.ZONDERVAN.COM

Contents

ACKNOWLEDGMENTS

This book is for anyone who has ever hoped to gain heavenly crowns.

God has blessed me with a faithful support team to create this book. They are the Alive Communications Literary Agency, Sandy Vander Zicht of Zondervan, and, most of all, my coauthor, Angela Hunt. Her talent and wisdom have enriched my dream of inspiring women to serve the Lord with more motivation.

Most of all, I wish to acknowledge the Lord for my family, especially my mother and my husband. Through them, he has taught me that serving him on earth is the greatest way to gain crowns in heaven.

Heather Whitestone McCallum

CHAPTER 1

AN UNEXPECTED
CROWN

I know a secret about you—something you may not have admitted even to yourself.

I know you'd like to wear a crown.

At one time or another, most of us would like to live out the Cinderella story. Often we see ourselves as the ugly duckling and pray for the day when we can become a royal swan.

You may know that I lost my hearing at the age of eighteen months. The powerful antibiotics that saved my life when I experienced a high fever also took my hearing. To take my mind off the endless rounds of therapy and training I had to endure, I dreamed of being a princess and a ballerina. I suppose every girl entertains such fantasies at some point because our parents read to us about princesses in fairy tales and fables and nursery rhymes. In such stories, the princess is always beautiful. She leads a life of luxury. Who wouldn't want that kind of life?

From that little deaf girl who dreamed of being a princess-ballerina, I grew into a young woman who set her sights on the most glittery tiara I had ever seen. Gathering my courage, I told my friends and family that I wanted to compete for the Miss America title, the most coveted crown in America.

Can you imagine their reaction? I was a deaf woman. I had never been a homecoming queen nor had I ever won any kind of pageant. My deafness had sheltered me from much of the world, and I had few hearing friends. Nothing in my personal history suggested that I would succeed. But I wanted to wear a crown more than anything. So I persevered.

The pageant itself was a nerve-wracking experience for all the contestants, but I was especially tense because I had no way of catching all the sounds around me. On that final night when I stood on the stage in Atlantic City with the other four finalists, I felt as if I were sitting on the top of a roller coaster, about to plunge to the earth. I had performed my ballet to the best of my ability, but who can predict the mind of a judge?

I had been nervous when I first met Regis Philbin, the emcee, a few days before. He was talking too fast for me to read his lips. Now I was wearing my hearing aid and trying to listen, but the noise and confusion swallowed up most of the announcements.

Regis announced that fourth runner-up was Tiffany Storm, Miss Indiana; third runner-up was Andrea Krahn, Miss Georgia; and second runner-up was Jennifer Makris, Miss New Jersey.

Miss Virginia, Cullen Johnson, stood beside me. Regis wasn't facing me, so I couldn't read his lips. I heard a buzzing and saw a wave of applause in the audience. I heard him say, "Miss Virginia," but I missed the other words. I didn't know if I had won or not. I kept thinking, *If Miss Virginia cries, she won,* but when I turned to look at her, Cullen was pointing at me.

Somehow I walked over to Kimberly Aiken, and she pinned the crown to my head. Someone handed me the Waterford Crystal scepter. I didn't realize I was holding it until I found it in my hand backstage. Pageant officials would have fainted if I had dropped it! From the corner of my eye I saw Kathie Lee Gifford applauding, tears in her eyes. Some automatic part of my consciousness propelled me toward the crowd. *Turn. Wave. Walk to the end of the runway. Turn again. Walk back to Kimberly.*

I pulled myself together as I moved down the runway and saw those lifted hands signing "I love you." I stood for a moment at the far end, overwhelmed by the cheering audience, and in my heart I cried out to God: *I really need you, Lord. You'd better come with me because I have no idea how I'm going to manage this . . .*

God did abide with me. On that night he gave me a physical crown. He stayed by my side through that stressful year—1995—and he has been with me ever since. My Lord Jesus has been my guide and comfort as I have married, given birth to two sons, and had a cochlear implant that dramatically improved my hearing.

He has given me so much, but I'm not done with earnestly desiring more—and now I want God's crowns more than anything in the world!

I hope you will come with me through these next pages as we explore the crowns prepared for those who believe in Christ. We will learn that the path to an incorruptible crown does not always lead us through wealth and fame and beauty, but often through the valley of the shadow. Just like Jesus, whose only earthly crown was made of thorns, we can travel from temptation to life, from the agony of despair to glorious victory.

One day we will stand before Jesus to receive crowns and rewards, but when the trials of everyday life crowd in—children, taxes, illness, work, finances, housing, wars and rumors of wars—it can be hard to take comfort in the joy to come when the frustration of the present is so overwhelming.

I am so happy to know that even these present days, dark though they may often be, are not without blessings. One day we will wear heavenly crowns, but Jesus has not left us without crowns in the present. These crowns are not literal, but figurative—unless, of course, you want to pick up a tiara on eBay to remind yourself that you are blessed to be a daughter of the King! Not a bad idea, is it?

Whether we realize it or not, God gives us a crown every day—the gift of living through Jesus Christ. God allows us to wake up every morning and breathe because he wants us to have an opportunity to be part of his beautiful family on earth and in heaven. He has given us miraculous bodies as treasures to glorify him. In return, God expects us to take good care of our bodies and our hearts, because daily he crowns us with his love and wants us to share his love with others.

Come with me as we further explore the wonderful crowns—earthly and heavenly—from Christ's infinite supply.

CHAPTER 2

CROWNS MEANT
FOR TODAY

*She will set a garland of grace on your head and present you
with a crown of splendor.*

Proverbs 4:9

E ver since I served as Miss America 1995, the word *crown* has
had a special meaning for me. My Miss America tiara is now
in my home, safely resting inside its velvet-lined box. I don't wear
it these days, but my boys like to peek at it every now and then.

For an entire year as I spoke to audiences nationwide, I wore
a crown-shaped rhinestone brooch on my suits. These days if I
wear a crown brooch, I'm more likely to be thinking of the present crowns in my life. Though I've come to see the Miss America
crown as a special blessing from God, I am now more interested
in the crowns God has in store for those who love and follow him.

An Ancient Glossary

The Old Testament uses a number of words that we translate
as "crown." The Hebrew word *ne'zer* refers to the plate of gold in
the front of the high priest's mitre and the diadem worn by Saul

in battle. Someone who wore this type of crown was set apart or consecrated for service. This crown was also used at the coronation of young King Joash. "Jehoiada brought out the king's son and put the crown on him; he presented him with a copy of the covenant and proclaimed him king" (2 Kings 11:12). This crown might have been made of silk or gold, inset with jewels. I can only imagine the seven-year-old boy flinching under the weight of a crown that carried a tremendous responsibility.

The Persian crown worn by the Hebrew Queen Esther was a *kether,* a high cap or tiara. This word also refers to ornaments worn at marriages, feasts, and festivals.[1]

Most Old Testament references to crowns come from the Hebrew word *atarah,* from the root "to encircle," as an army would encircle a city. These are the head ornaments worn by kings from many nations. This word is used a number of times in the book of Proverbs to describe crowns available to godly men and women.

The Garland of Grace

I love reading Solomon's proverbs because they contain so much information on how to live a practical, godly life. Solomon—a king himself who certainly had one or more crowns of his own—didn't write much about heaven, but he wrote of many figurative crowns that we can wear here on earth.

The wisest man who ever lived had much to say about the first crown you can win and wear today:

Do not forsake wisdom, and she will protect you; love her, and she will watch over you. Wisdom is supreme; therefore get wisdom. Though it cost all you have, get understanding. Esteem her, and she will exalt you; embrace her, and she will honor you. She will set a garland of grace on your head and present you with a crown of splendor.

Proverbs 4:6–9

Would you like the events of your daily life to be crowned with grace and splendor? Then follow Solomon's advice and seek wisdom! Wisdom will guard your words and your steps. Her cousin, understanding, will exalt you. What woman wouldn't like to be known as a fountain of perceptive insight?

But take care where you seek wisdom. Do not seek human wisdom, particularly from those who demonstrate their own foolishness by denying God. ("The fool says in his heart, 'There is no God'" [Psalm 14:1].) Seek the wisdom of God through prayer, through the study of his Word, and through the counsel of godly people.

And remember this: Wisdom is not the same thing as knowledge. You could be a walking encyclopedia and earn ten doctoral degrees and still be unwise. Nor is wisdom the same as intelligence. You may be able to solve every mathematic, spatial, or word problem presented to you in a matter of seconds and still lack wisdom.

I know some wonderful people who never went to college and couldn't begin to solve an algebraic equation, but when I have a problem, they're the first ones I call for advice. Why? Because they have wisdom and don't view the world through man's eyes; rather, they have learned to consider situations from God's eternal perspective. If you can learn to see the world in the light of eternity, you will be wiser than any college professor who cannot see and will not acknowledge that God created the universe and rules in the affairs of men.

The Bible gives us a precious promise: "If any of you lacks wisdom, he should ask God, who gives generously to all without finding fault, and it will be given to him" (James 1:5).

If you want to be crowned with a garland of grace, ask the Lord for wisdom—and learn to see your world through the eyes of Christ.

The Crown of Blessing

Solomon wrote of another crown available to you today: "Blessings crown the head of the righteous, but violence overwhelms the mouth of the wicked" (Proverbs 10:6).

If you want your life and your family to be crowned with blessing, live a righteous life. In other words, choose to walk with God so you will do good and not evil. When tempted to lie, tell the truth instead. When you are tempted to steal, refuse. When you are tempted to gossip or hate your neighbor, choose to do good and exhibit kindness. Study the words of Christ and follow his example.

By looking at the world, you can see that violence results in more violence, gossip spawns more gossip, pain causes more pain. If you will choose to do good and teach your children to be kind, you and your family are likely to enjoy a life of blessing for as long as you live on earth.

The Crown of Wealth

A few years ago, a book called *The Millionaire Next Door* became a runaway best seller.[2] The authors, Drs. Thomas Stanley and William Danko, discovered that most American millionaires weren't Donald Trump-types at all. They were quiet people who drove older cars, invested wisely, and worked hard. They were frugal folks who shopped at Sears and J.C. Penney and bought clothes off the rack. They were wise with their money. As a result, they were crowned with wealth.

Solomon understood this principle. He wrote, "The wealth of the wise is their crown, but the folly of fools yields folly" (Proverbs 14:24). His life illustrated this proverb; he was not only one of the wisest men who ever lived, but he was also one of the richest!

We must remember though that the Bible never guarantees that children of God will be rich. I do not believe God wants all of us to be wealthy. If we had no material needs, we might grow complacent and forget about God.

On another occasion Solomon wrote: "Keep falsehood and lies far from me; give me neither poverty nor riches, but give me only my daily bread. Otherwise, I may have too much and disown you and say, 'Who is the Lord?' Or I may become poor and steal, and so dishonor the name of my God" (Proverbs 30:8–9).

Although God has not promised to make us rich, he has promised to provide for our needs. And when our wills are in tune with his, he grants the desires of our hearts.

In a college class one day, a fellow student said she visited a psychic to learn about her future. The fortune-teller had told her she would marry a wealthy man and have a big, beautiful house with lots of children.

I looked at my classmate and envied her dream. I even considered seeing the psychic because I wanted to hear that one day I would live like a princess in a palace. I thought it would be wonderful to have a rich husband and never have to work. I loved big houses and thought of being a mom.

But I was a Christian, and the Spirit of God told me it would be wrong to visit a psychic. He spoke to my heart and asked, *Who would you rather trust with your future, me or some strange woman?* In that moment I knew I needed to obey God and remain in the center of his will.

I don't know if my fellow student ever married a rich man and moved into a big house. But I am glad I never followed in her footsteps because today I feel every inch a princess. My husband is not rich and I have to work part-time; however, the Lord has blessed us with a three-bedroom house and a two-acre yard, a pony and a chocolate lab for my boys to enjoy. The house is not a mansion, and those two acres require a lot of mowing!

But I feel like a princess because having my husband and two sons makes me feel truly blessed. We have learned not to measure our success by how many things we own, but by how much of a difference we make in other people's lives. One hundred years from now, no one will remember how much power or money we had—but our great-grandchildren will remember how much we loved our children and how often we talked about Jesus.

A friend of mine recently attended a funeral for Dean, a quiet Christian man. He never taught a Sunday school class, never preached a sermon, never wrote a book, but he treated people honestly and with fairness. He loved his wife and his four sons, and he loved God. And when he died, the church was packed with people who appreciated all Dean had quietly said and done.

His wife wrote a list of ten things he would never have to say about his life. One of them was that he will never have to say he wanted more because he always said he had more than enough.

Isn't that a wonderful testimony? Paul warned young Timothy about men who preach that religion is a means to wealth. Such men, Paul wrote, "have been robbed of the truth and ... think that godliness is a means to financial gain. But godliness with contentment is great gain. For we brought nothing into the world, and we can take nothing out of it" (1 Timothy 6:5–7).

So when it comes to money, remember this: If you are foolish, you will watch as your money sprouts wings and flies away. If you are wise enough to see and act through God's perspective, you may enjoy a crown of wealth.

And if you follow Christ, you will always have more than enough.

The Crown of Splendor

Janet White was one of my role models when I was preparing for the Miss Alabama Pageant. She was my college professor at the time, and I remember her reading God's words like a hungry deer drinking the river. Whenever I visited her, she shared her wisdom with me.

One day we were talking about silver hair. I don't remember how the subject came up, but I found it interesting to know that God considers silver hair a beautiful crown. Solomon wrote, "Gray hair is a crown of splendor; it is attained by a righteous life" (Proverbs 16:31). It's unfortunate that many people today don't see gray hair in the same light. So much strength, wisdom, and beauty resides in our elders.

A few days ago I was in my study working on my computer. My two active toddlers were knocking the books off the shelves, so my babysitter, Mattie, came in to help me clean up the mess. She saw a copy of my most recent book, *Let God Surprise You*. The cover—a young ballerina silhouetted against a cloudy horizon—reminded her of her childhood on a farm in south Georgia. "Back then I dreamed of being a mother and having eight children."

That much of Mattie's dream came true, but her husband abandoned her with eight children when the youngest was only a few years old. To feed her kids, she worked a full-time job. This meant sacrificing her time with her children, though she was careful to take time to share God's love with her little ones. Mattie has never been bitter about her difficult life. Even now that her children are grown, she continues to faithfully serve children and exhibit God's love.

One day Mattie showed me a rhinestone tiara she had just purchased. She planned to surprise her eighty-year-old mother with the crown on her birthday. Mattie said she and all the children and grandchildren would declare her mother "Queen of the Birthday."

I couldn't help feeling a little envious of that eighty-year-old mother. I would be honored if my children do something similar when my hair is crowned in shimmering silver.

The Crown of Grandchildren

Wise Solomon also wrote that "Children's children are a crown to the aged, and parents are the pride of their children" (Proverbs 17:6).

I'm too young for grandchildren at this point, but I can see how much my little ones are loved by their grandparents. I often hear grandparents joke about how this is the most special time of life because they get to play with the babies and then send the children back to their parents when it's time for discipline or cleaning up!

I believe grandchildren are a living crown. Unlike my Miss America crown, which cannot dance with me or cheer me up, grandchildren can lighten your heart and thrill your soul.

My grandmother is always delighted to see me, and I enjoy visiting with her. I think she was more excited about my winning Miss America than my mother was! She now has a circle of ten grandchildren and eleven great-grandchildren, and she loves cooking for all of us on holidays.

If you have been blessed with children, you may have the crown of grandchildren waiting in your future. If you raise your children in love and faith, you can look forward to the day when you have the opportunity to share that same love and faith with your grandchildren.

You Can *Be* a Crown!

Still speaking figuratively, Solomon wrote that not only do righteous people have access to crowns, but married women also have the opportunity to *be* a crown! In Proverbs 12:4 he wrote, "A wife of noble character is her husband's crown, but a disgraceful wife is like decay in his bones."

Recently a friend's daughter received a diamond on her twenty-second birthday. When my husband, John, heard the news, he said something about the girl being too young to be engaged. "But John," I reminded him, "I was twenty-two when you asked me to marry you!"

This prompted me to think about all I have accomplished over the past few years. I've given birth to two wonderful boys, published four books, served on the President's Committee of the Employment of People with Disabilities, and am now an advisory board member of the National Institute of Health for Deafness. Plus there was that little thing of dancing on live television and winning the Miss America crown . . . While my brain spun around all my accomplishments, the Holy Spirit jolted me with a dose of reality. *What was I doing, thinking so much of myself? I was no longer just Heather Whitestone, Miss America; I was also Mrs. Heather McCallum, wife and mother.*

In the past few months, I had been so focused on myself and my career that I had not been thinking of my sons and my husband. I had not called a music teacher or a church group to see about involving my boys in programs they would enjoy; when a speaking opportunity for me had come up, I had merely called the babysitter and taken off. My husband was running for public office, but I did not volunteer to help him with phone calls or meeting people.

Oh, how foolish I had been. I had been focused on myself rather than on being a crown of blessing for my children and my husband.

Immediately, my heart changed. I asked God to guide me so I could reach out and be what John needed as he ran for office. I made phone calls and went with him to meet his contributors and supporters. I asked them if there was anything I could do to help them help John. I tried to be more like a servant than a star.

If we cultivate and exhibit noble character, we will be our husband's crowns. If we bring disgrace to our husbands, we will ultimately destroy them.

What is noble character for a wife? Solomon wrote a lot about the virtues of womanhood (see Proverbs 31), but one of the most important things a Christian wife can do is heed the advice of Proverbs 14:1: "The wise woman builds her house, but with her own hands the foolish one tears hers down."

How does a wise woman build her house? By building up her husband and children, surrounding them with love and acceptance and devotion.

How does a foolish woman destroy her house? Not by literally knocking down walls but by tearing down her husband and children with harsh words and stinging rebuke. When you must correct your children, speak with love and firm guidance. If you must correct your husband, do so in private and speak in gentle terms. Never criticize your husband in public; do not belittle him before other family or friends. If you are honest with your husband—speaking the truth in love and supporting him in public—you will become his crowning glory!

Looking Ahead . . .

The crowns we have discussed so far aren't the only blessings the Christian experiences in this life—we have forgiveness for sin, mercy, and grace. We have a heavenly Father who listens to our prayers; a Savior who intercedes for us; and a Spirit who comforts, teaches, guides, and convicts. The Spirit even prays for us when we are so distressed that we can't find the right words (see Romans 8:26).

We will experience rewards in heaven too—eternal life, fullness of joy, the treasures we have laid up where neither moth nor rust nor thieves can destroy (Matthew 6:19). We will have supernatural bodies that will never age, weaken, or get sick. We will behold the glory of God and the face of Christ. We will shine like the stars and enter into mansions the Savior has prepared for us.

And we will receive rewards—crowns of honor that will never fade or wither or break.

CHAPTER 3

A HEAVENLY CONTEST

*I am thinking today of that beautiful land
I shall reach when life's sun goeth down.
When through wonderful grace by my Savior I'll stand
Will there be any stars in my crown?*

Eliza E. Hewitt

In the New Testament, two Greek words are translated as "crown." *Diadema* refers to a king's crown and symbolizes power to rule. *Stephanos* refers to a wreath of victory, honor, or reward worn by Romans and Greeks. The wreath-like crowns worn by winners in the Olympic games were made of wild olive leaves; other contests awarded victory crowns made of laurel, parsley, or pine. But athletes were not the only people rewarded with crowns; the Romans bestowed a "civic crown" of oak leaves to anyone who saved a citizen's life.

The biblical writers were well acquainted with the idea of these "living" crowns. But plants die, leaves droop, and branches break. In contrast to these temporary crowns, the apostles wrote of crowns—heavenly crowns—that would not fade, wither, or deteriorate. These crowns would last forever. Peter wrote, "Praise be to the God and Father of our Lord Jesus Christ! In his great mercy he has given us new birth into a living hope through the resurrection of Jesus Christ from the dead, and into an inheritance that can never perish, spoil or fade—kept in heaven for you" (1 Peter 1:3–4).

For many years after I accepted Christ, I was content to know that I would go to heaven after I died—and that was good enough for me! Lately, though, I have taken an interest in learning more about things that will happen at the end of the world as we know it. I have come to realize that "just" going to heaven isn't good enough for me. Showing up in heaven empty handed would be like going to a birthday party for a beloved friend and being the only one who forgot to bring a present for the guest of honor!

One day we will stand before Jesus, who himself promised that "the Son of Man is going to come in his Father's glory with his angels, and then he will reward each person according to what he has done" (Matthew 16:27). The heavenly crowns are part of our rewards.

Do you know what the best news is about specific heavenly crowns (which we will name and discuss in later chapters)? Unlike the Miss America tiara, which is given to only one young woman per year, these heavenly crowns are available to everyone who follows Christ! As Rita Bennet notes, "This race of living our lives to glorify Christ is different from the ones run in the Atlanta Olympics or in a school meet, because here we are not striving to beat out the other runners. Rather, our motivation is to do the best for God's sake. In a spiritual race each one can win."[1]

As I've studied heaven and its crowns of honor, the thought of one particular event thrills me . . .

The Victory Stand for Believers

I look forward to the day when I stand before the judgment seat of Christ, also known as the bema judgment. The Greek word *bema* was originally used to describe the elevated seat on which the judge of an athletic contest would sit. The athletes who had lost the contest would not even get near the bema seat; this was a place of acknowledgement and reward for the victors only. Likewise, the judgment seat of Christ is not for unbelievers. This judgment is for Christians alone—believers who have come to Christ during what is known as the "church age."

As a child, I used to think that God sat up in heaven and wrote down every bad thing I ever did. Even after I became a Christian (when I thought he might begin to write down at least a few *good* things), I thought I would still have to pay for those bad things.

Do you know that my sins—all the bad things I have ever done—have already been washed away? Jesus' death paid for all my sins, past, present, and future. When I stand before the bema seat, God will see me as his beloved, cleansed from sin, washed whiter than snow. Hebrews 8:12 assures us, "For I will forgive their wickedness and will remember their sins no more."

So what will happen at this event? We will see or experience a review of our words, deeds, and attitudes. Jesus said, "There is nothing concealed that will not be disclosed, or hidden that will not be made known. What you have said in the dark will be heard in the daylight, and what you have whispered in the ear in the inner rooms will be proclaimed from the roofs" (Luke 12:2–3).

What will be judged and by whom? "For we must all appear before the judgment seat of Christ, that each one may receive what is due him for the things done while in the body, whether good or bad" (2 Corinthians 5:10). Our earthly accomplishments will be judged by none other than our Lord Jesus, who said that "the Father judges no one, but has entrusted all judgment to the Son" (John 5:22).

When will this judgment occur? Prophecy teacher Dwight Pentecost points out that 1 Corinthians 4:5; 2 Timothy 4:8; and Revelation 22:12 associate the reward with "that day"—in which Christ comes for his own.[2] Jesus said, "Behold, I am coming soon! My reward is with me, and I will give to everyone according to what he has done" (Revelation 22:12).

Yes, the judgment culminates with the giving of rewards, including crowns.

The Judge's Standards

How will the Lord judge our works? According to whether they magnified God—or brought glory only to ourselves.

For centuries children learning the fundamentals of the Christian faith have memorized a catechism question: "What is the chief end of man?" And its simple answer, "To glorify God and to enjoy him forever," is another way of stating what Paul wrote in 1 Corinthians 10:31. "So whether you eat or drink or whatever you do, do it all for the glory of God."

When the Lord tests our works through a purifying fire, actions that reflected glory to God will be revealed as gold or precious stones; actions intended to make us look good will become worthless ash.

Dwight Pentecost explains that it is "not the Lord's purpose here to chasten His child for his sins, but to reward his service for those things done in the name of the Lord."[3] The glorification of God is the "bottom line" in this judgment, but there are other criteria by which our works will be evaluated, including how we have treated other believers:

> Anyone who receives a prophet because he is a prophet will receive a prophet's reward, and anyone who receives a righteous man because he is a righteous man will receive a righteous man's reward. And if anyone gives even a cup of cold water to one of these little ones because he is my disciple, I tell you the truth, he will certainly not lose his reward.
>
> Matthew 10:41–42

If you treat a minister, a fellow Christian, or even a child with Christian love, you will be rewarded. If, however, you have grudgingly offered help to your brothers and sisters in Christ, your works will vanish in a puff of smoke.

We will also be judged on how well we exercised our God-given gifts. To illustrate this, in Luke 19 Jesus told the story of a nobleman who called ten of his servants and gave them each a measure of money (a pound of silver, known as a *mina*). The nobleman then went away to be crowned king. When the king returned, the first servant presented himself and gave his report, that he had invested the mina so that it had earned ten times its value. "Well done, my good servant!" the king replied. "Because you have been trustworthy in a very small matter, take charge of ten cities."

A second servant reported a fivefold increase on the investment. For this the king gave him responsibility over five cities. Another servant reported that he had not invested the money. Motivated by fear, he had hid it in the linen closet.

> His master replied, "I will judge you by your own words, you wicked servant! You knew, did you, that I am a hard man, taking out what I did not put in, and reaping what I did not sow? Why then didn't you put my money on deposit, so that when I came back, I could have collected it with interest?"
>
> Then he said to those standing by, "Take his mina away from him and give it to the one who has ten minas."
>
> "Sir," they said, "he already has ten!"
>
> He replied, "I tell you that to everyone who has, more will be given, but as for the one who has nothing, even what he has will be taken away."
>
> Luke 19:22–26

A Time of Rejoicing, Not Tears

We should look forward to the judgment seat of Christ because we will rejoice to receive heavenly rewards, including crowns. Many people have wondered what they'll look like and whether they'll be literal or metaphorical objects.

The author of Revelation describes twenty-four elders (who represent the church) laying their crowns before Christ's throne (4:10). That passage seems to suggest that they are literal objects.

Even if they are literal, however, they are certainly symbolic. Just as my wedding ring symbolizes my love for and commitment to my husband, these crowns symbolize our determination and desire to glorify Jesus.

When Jesus told the parable about the man who used his gifts wisely and was placed in charge of "ten cities," he seemed to indicate that our rewards will be increased responsibilities. Bible teacher Harold Willmington writes, "It has been suggested that these 'crowns' will be talents and abilities with which to glorify Christ. Thus, the greater the reward, the greater the ability."[4] So if you have ever wanted to sing like Sandi Patty or preach like Franklin Graham, your desires may be fulfilled in heaven.

I'm sure all of us will feel regret when some of our deeds crumble into ashes, but we will be honored to learn how little things we did—perhaps actions so small we promptly forgot about them—brought glory to God.

A woman recently told me a story about her college days. One Valentine's Day her boyfriend, living in another city, sent her a dozen red roses in a stunning vase. She was thrilled with the thoughtfulness and the gift, but she had to go out of town and knew she couldn't take the roses with her.

An older widow lived in the dorm as a housemother of sorts. Thinking the woman might not have received roses in years, this student took the roses to the widow's room, knocked on the door, and hurried away before she could be discovered.

That was an unselfish and generous act, right? It was the sort of thing that would bless an older woman's heart and bring glory to God—but I'm not finished with the story.

The student then called her boyfriend and told him what she'd done. That wasn't wrong in itself, but, she confessed to me, "The minute I hung up the phone, I knew that I had told him about giving the flowers away because I wanted him to think I was generous. And in that moment, I realized that what had once been a good deed was now absolutely worthless in the sight of God because I used it for my own personal gain."

Jesus knew about our sinful tendencies and cautioned us about giving gifts with ulterior motives:

> When you give to the needy, do not announce it with trumpets, as the hypocrites do in the synagogues and on the streets, to be honored by men. I tell you the truth, they have received their reward in full. But when you give to the needy, do not let your left hand know what your right hand is doing, so that your giving may be in secret. Then your Father, who sees what is done in secret, will reward you.
>
> Matthew 6:2–4

Do Not Be Weary in Doing Good

Sometimes we become discouraged and feel we are not being rewarded for all our work. Or we think our efforts do not make much difference; surely we will receive the same heavenly rewards as everyone else. This is what Satan wants you to believe, because he does not want you to share your faith or continue to glorify God through your works.

God, on the other hand, understands our motivational needs. He is like a father who promises to give his children an allowance if they rake the yard. As they work, the father watches closely. He sees that one child rakes the entire yard while the other rakes only one flower bed. When they are welcomed back into the house, he crowns them both with love, but he gives the hardest-working child a bigger allowance.

You may think your life is too ordinary to be of eternal significance, but we never know how our smallest actions can ripple out to affect others. Oswald Chambers wrote, "My personal life may be crowded with small petty incidents, altogether unnoticeable and mean; but if I obey Jesus Christ in the haphazard circumstances, they become pinholes through which I see the face of God, and when I stand face to face with God I will discover that through my obedience thousands were blessed."[5]

When I hear from a woman who feels she cannot serve God in her "insignificant" position, I think of the people who helped Annie, born in April 1866 to an alcoholic father and a mother with tuberculosis. At age five, Annie contracted trachoma, a disease of the eye. With no money for doctors, Annie's disease went untreated. She gradually lost her vision.

Her mother died. Because her father could not support a family, Annie was sent to relatives, but she and her brother ended up in the state poorhouse. Here she was, ten years old and living with the mentally ill, prostitutes, and others whom society had cast off.

When her beloved brother died, the only thing Annie could cling to was the dream of education. She had heard of schools for the blind and desperately wanted to attend one. When an investigating committee visited the poorhouse, Annie begged to be sent to school. Supported by the generous giving of Christians, a few months later Annie enrolled at the Perkins Institute for the Blind in Boston.

Annie arrived at the school with strong determination and an equally strong will. She rebelled at first, snapping the patience of her teachers and her classmates, but not every teacher gave up on her. Several saw a quick intellect in the untamed girl, and many of them persevered with her. After beginning school at age fourteen on the elementary level, Annie graduated as valedictorian at age twenty.

Not long after graduation, Annie learned of a deaf and blind student in Alabama who needed a teacher. Annie accepted the position and in time she opened the world to Helen Keller. Together, Anne Sullivan and Helen helped the entire world see the possibilities locked away inside a disabled body.

I don't know if the people who financially supported Annie's education ever saw the astounding results of their dedication, but I am sure they learned the good news after entering heaven. And at the bema seat, when they stand before Christ, they will be rewarded for faithful service.

So let's live righteous lives and seek to glorify God, not ourselves, in all we do. As Amy Carmichael wrote, "We will have all of eternity to celebrate the victories, and only a few hours before sunset in which to win them."[6]

In later chapters, we'll discuss five scripturally identified heavenly crowns for "special service." But first I want to look at a very earthly crown, worn by our Lord and Savior—and Judge—Jesus Christ.

CHAPTER 4

THE CROWN
OF THORNS

O sacred Head, now wounded,
With grief and shame weighed down,
Now scornfully surrounded
With thorns, thine only crown!
O sacred Head, what glory,
What bliss, till now was thine!
Yet, though despised and gory,
I joy to call thee mine.

Bernard of Clairvaux

Jesus, the glorious King of kings and Lord of lords, suffered greatly during his time on earth. You are probably familiar with the story of his crucifixion and the terrible agony of his death, but have you considered the other things he suffered?

The baby who should have been cradled by angels and honored by kings was born to a poor carpenter and laid in a feed box for animals. The son who should have worn the finest clothing the world had to offer wore rough fabrics and simple sandals. The prophet who should have been received with awe and wonder was reviled and criticized. The rabbi who should have been allowed to teach in the most highly regarded synagogues was often forced to speak on hillsides and stony mountains. The leader who should have won unfailing devotion from his followers was betrayed, denied, and abandoned.

His cousin was beheaded. His good friend Lazarus died. His followers fell away. The multitudes who waved palm branches and joyfully received him vanished. The people he yearned to guide and protect scattered when he looked at them with blood running down his brow.

I'm sure there were occasions when Jesus felt like the loneliest man on earth. He had no wife to comfort him, no children to fill his heart, and many of his relatives believed him insane.

Because he had the very heart and mind of God, Jesus suffered agonies about which we can only speculate. The compassion and knowledge of God are so far above and beyond our comprehension, I can't even begin to imagine the cruel anguish Jesus experienced as he became sin for us.

He suffered beyond anything we can experience—and we are called to follow in his footsteps. But we will be compensated for our suffering, rewarded far beyond our expectation or imagining. "I tell you the truth," Jesus said, "no one who has left home or brothers or sisters or mother or father or children or fields for me and the gospel will fail to receive a hundred times as much in this present age (homes, brothers, sisters, mothers, children and fields—and with them, persecutions) and in the age to come, eternal life" (Mark 10:29–30).

Please understand this—the crown of thorns is *not* one of the heavenly crowns that will be bestowed on us. This is Jesus' crown, which he has already worn (Matthew 27:29). But it is important that we consider the crown of thorns because our response to suffering is one of the things Christ will consider when we stand before the bema seat.

The Fellowship of Jesus' Sufferings

Harold Willmington learned about the sufferings of Christians when he was a student at Moody Bible Institute in 1952. He had purchased a beautiful wall plaque imprinted with Philippians 3:10 (KJV): "That I may know him, and the power of his resurrection." Willmington was so proud of and inspired by the words on this sign. It became the first object he looked at when he woke up in the morning, and the last sight he saw before going to bed. He was so fond of the passage that he had decided to make it his "life's verse."

But one day a friend came into his dorm room, saw the plaque, admired it, but informed Willmington that the verse was incomplete. Somewhat shocked, Willmington looked up the verse in his Bible. After discovering the entire message, he suddenly became less sure he wanted this as his life's verse: "That I may know him, and the power of his resurrection, and the fellowship of his sufferings, being made conformable unto his death."

As Willmington explained it,

You see, I had been tremendously inspired by the first part of the verse, but was definitely less excited about the second section. I wanted the power of the resurrection without the fellowship of the sufferings, but this is impossible! One simply cannot have the first apart from the second![1]

Don't Buy the Lie

Beware of anyone who tells you that the Christian life is sheer bliss and one continuous bed of roses. Yes, Christians can and do experience abiding joy, often even in the darkest of circumstances. We have hope in situations where others have none. We have peace when the world roils in confusion. We have all these things because we have Jesus, who *is* joy and hope and peace.

But we are called to follow the Savior and pick up our cross—bear what he calls us to bear—and even though Jesus helps us bear the pain, sometimes the cross is heavy. At various times we may suffer physical pain, experience loneliness, and endure crippling anguish.

My babies were both born healthy, but I have read about devoted Christian women whose infants were born with fatal illnesses, and I cannot imagine how they suffered.

I have known families who lost teenage children in car accidents. I have watched them grieve and felt my heart twist with sympathy for their pain.

Suffering is part of life, even a Christian life, but the difference in our experience is that we will be rewarded for our suffering. God can take the greatest pain and use it for his glory and good.

In a later chapter I will talk about the suffering of persecuted Christians around the world. In this chapter, however, I want to explore the personal pain you and I sometimes experience.

The other day a friend told me about a prayer she offers for young couples getting married. "I pray that they will find joy and happiness," she said, "but I also wish them a measured dose of sorrow. Shared grief is powerful enough to create an unbreakable union." Pain teaches us that we are weak—but God's strength is limitless.

When we come to the end of our own ability and strength and power and talents, only then are we totally dependent on God. God wants us to depend on him. He does not want us to live good lives by our own power; he wants us to live supernatural lives through the power of his Son.

The world is full of independent people who are living examples of what people think Christians should and should not be. These folks go to church regularly, tithe, and pray over their meals. They don't curse, drink, or go to bad movies. They are fine examples of what the world expects Christians to be.

Yet when sorrow strikes, these folks are often completely at a loss. They have been living by their own power, and Jesus has had very little to do with their lives. In times of stress and struggle, their faith is tested—and often they will either abandon it or cry out to the Savior. If in brokenness they call on Jesus, he will meet them and prove his all-sufficiency.

Physical Suffering

Are you suffering today? You may be suffering physically. The apostle Paul, whose prayers shook heaven, prayed that the Lord would take away a physical ailment he called his "thorn in the flesh." We're not sure what it was—some say it was poor eyesight, some think it might have been migraine headaches. But whatever it was, three times Paul asked the Lord to take his suffering away, and three times God said no.

But he said to me, "My grace is sufficient for you, for my power is made perfect in weakness." Therefore I will boast all the more gladly about my weaknesses, so that Christ's power may rest on me. That is why, for Christ's sake, I delight in weaknesses, in insults, in hardships, in persecutions, in difficulties. For when I am weak, then I am strong.

2 Corinthians 12:7–10

Paul learned that his "thorn in the flesh" was part of God's will for his life. That condition—whatever it was—kept him dependent on the strength of God.

I have a condition that keeps me dependent on God too—I've had to depend on God for hearing. Motherhood has made me yearn for two working ears.

You may already know that in the fall of 2002 I had a cochlear implant that helped me hear through my right ear for the first time in twenty-eight years. Since I was eighteen months old, my right ear has been totally deaf and I could hear from my left ear only with the help of a hearing aid.

One day that summer I saw my husband rush outside to help my son John-John, who was crying. I hadn't heard my son call for help. John-John was okay, but realizing that I hadn't heard him distressed me and prompted me to seriously investigate having a cochlear implant.

When the device was activated, *Good Morning America* taped the event. I told a national television audience that I believed God would bless me with a new sound every day. I couldn't hear my boys at first—when the cochlear device is first activated, the result is like hearing a radio station broadcasting in a foreign language. I could hear all the sounds, but I couldn't understand them.

In the first two days, I heard the sounds of hands clapping and running water. Speech was too complicated for my brain to process at that time, but I believed God would help me learn to sort out all the sounds. I knew the world was waiting and watching. For a few weeks after the activation of my device, I gave several interviews to the media. I loved being an example of how the Nucleus device—which had been invented by a Christian doctor—could help people find more enjoyment and fulfillment in life.

I was expecting a period of adjustment followed by happiness. I had no idea I was headed for a period of some of the most intense suffering I had ever known.

Emotional Suffering

A few weeks later, when the wave of media interest had subsided, I was home alone with my two boys, who are one and two years old. I discovered that living with a cochlear implant made me feel more tired than usual; my brain was overwhelmed with new sounds and it took effort to decipher them. On top of all the new sounds, I had to deal with two active and sometimes fussy boys.

One day everything just seemed to pile up and collapse on top of me. My family members were all at work so I couldn't call anyone for help. My mood veered from depression to discouragement to anger—why wasn't someone coming to help me?

My boys refused to go to bed for their naps. They began to test me. I tried to handle them and couldn't. Then I tried to close my eyes and rest, but I couldn't relax; my brain was roiling with thoughts and sounds and frustration. And I knew I couldn't go to sleep; my little ones were running around with no one else to watch them.

My boys screamed at me and each other, fighting over their toys. Their screams felt like hammers banging against my brain, and finally I lost my temper and cursed. I wanted to grab my little boys and shake them, but the Spirit spoke to my heart and begged me not to be too hard on them. They were too little to understand what was happening to me.

When John came home from work that day, he couldn't understand my negative attitude. He clearly wasn't happy about coming home to a complaining wife, and I couldn't blame him for feeling that way.

I took a long look at myself. I still couldn't hear better, and I felt totally guilty because I was becoming bitter. I hated myself. With my bitterness and foolishness, I was destroying everything I wanted to build. *I'm just not good enough to be a mother,* I thought.

Yearning for quiet, I went into the backyard and turned off my hearing aid and the cochlear device. Sitting in complete and welcome silence, I remembered my difficult childhood—the thousands of therapy sessions in which I had learned how to speak and interpret sounds from my hearing aid.

In a way, I was starting over. I didn't really want to start over—I'd had enough speech and auditory training as a child to last ten lifetimes—but the auditory therapists I contacted strongly believed I should attend sessions two to five days per week. But how could I manage that kind of work when I had responsibilities to my children, my husband, and my speaking career? And auditory therapy is not inexpensive—added to that, I had to pay for babysitters every time I went to therapy.

To make matters worse, in my recent public appearances I had practically invited the world to watch while God blessed me with new sounds. Ha! What would the world think if they saw me sitting here, stressed out and in tears, with both my cochlear device and my hearing aid turned off?

I had expected tears of rejoicing. What I tasted were tears of defeat. I begged God to take me to heaven and give my responsibilities to another deaf woman who could handle them better. I thought I could not bear the responsibility of raising godly sons and being a role model while my attitude was so rotten at home.

I was at the bottom of a pit and wanted to stay there. I wanted John and the boys to go on without me. Surely they would be better off if they had a hearing wife and mother who would be more fun and not cross and frustrated so much of the time . . .

I wish I could tell you that the clouds rolled back and God boomed reassurance from heaven, but that didn't happen. I remained terribly depressed for several days, and my frustrations with my new hearing didn't magically vanish. My step-mother-in-law told me she was concerned because my boys, visiting her home, told her I was sad. As little as they were, they were depressed too.

One afternoon not long after my quiet time in the garden, I saw my boys standing in the hallway. They looked so young . . . so vulnerable, just like I had been as a child. And then God spoke to my heart, reminding me of the time when I was in high school and my parents got a divorce. After that, I had begged God to bless me with a healthy family because I did not ever want my children to endure what I had suffered.

Looking at my boys, I suddenly realized that they were just as sad and confused as I was when I first heard that my parents were divorcing. The Spirit led me to my Bible, where I read Proverbs 17:22: "A cheerful heart is good medicine, but a crushed spirit dries up the bones."

In that moment, I knew I needed a cheerful heart—and I needed help. I had been a crushed spirit for too long. Almost immediately, I went to a medical doctor to check on my health. I also went to a Christian counselor for two months. These professionals helped me keep my head above the dark waters that had threatened to drown me.

In the next chapter, I'll share with you some personal practices that helped relieve my emotional and spiritual turmoil.

Spiritual Suffering

Christian novelist Athol Dickson has encountered some dark times in his life; recently, he nursed his mother through a year-long illness that ended in her death. Through the sorrow of losing a woman he loved profoundly, Athol found his faith tested—and wanting.

No miracle came to save his mother. The doctors could offer no hope. And even though his mom knew she would soon be meeting Jesus in heaven, Athol grew angry at God. For months Athol says he lived without any sense of God's presence. And for the first time he considered the possibility that everything he had believed about God was a lie. Spiritually, he stepped into a place he describes as "nothingness."

> One of the marvelous things about grief is the way it strips away distractions. The complete lack of meaning in that place left me with nowhere to hide. Only one obvious fact

remained: Life is pointless if God does not exist. When I realized that, when I was finally ready to give God my full attention, he imposed himself upon me for the one and only time. He asked a question I thought I had already answered years ago: "Do you want me even at the cost of a cross to bear, or do you want to cling to the equivocations that led you here?"

Standing at the edge of nothingness, without even self-pity left for comfort, the answer seemed obvious. I wanted my Daddy![2]

In that place of earnest need, Athol Dickson learned that faith is not easy or cheap. He was reminded of the man who came to Jesus and begged, "I do believe; help me overcome my unbelief!" (Mark 9:24). "This is grace versus works at its most fundamental level," Athol says. "I am saved by grace through faith, but I get faith through grace."

In that place of nothingness brought on by suffering, Athol found a turning point. "Do you want?" Jesus asked. When we are at peace and content with life, it is so easy to answer yes. When we are suffering and torn apart by sorrow, it is much harder to reach out with trembling hands and embrace the Savior.

Being a Christian means sometimes wearing a crown of suffering. Sometimes we will weep—and sometimes we will feel utterly broken. Sometimes you may walk around with a smiling face pasted over a heart that fills like a water balloon—one little prick, and you will spill your tears in a flood.

And as Athol concludes, "Still . . . I would much rather face life with Jesus than without him. And because I turned away from him for part of that last year with my mother I can now honestly say that I would choose the suffering of this life with him rather than any life without him because when I turned away in anger, the emptiness I felt was the worst kind of suffering."[3]

Oswald Chambers noted that sometimes God speaks most profoundly to us in those dark nights of the soul: "There are times in the life of every disciple when things are not clear or easy, when it is not possible to know what to do or say. Such times of darkness come as a discipline to the character and as the means of fuller knowledge of the Lord. Such darkness is a time for listening, not for speaking. This aspect of darkness as a necessary side to fellowship with God is not unusual in the Bible" (see Isaiah 5:30, 50:10 and 1 Peter 1:6–7).[4]

We Will Be Rewarded for Suffering

Paul explains that suffering is something all creation endures as a result of sin:

> Now if we are children, then we are heirs—heirs of God and co-heirs with Christ, if indeed we share in his sufferings in order that we may also share in his glory.
>
> I consider that our present sufferings are not worth comparing with the glory that will be revealed in us. The creation waits in eager expectation for the sons of God to be revealed . . . We know that the whole creation has been groaning as in the pains of childbirth right up to the present time. Not only so, but we ourselves, who have the firstfruits of the Spirit, groan inwardly as we wait eagerly for our adoption as sons, the redemption of our bodies.
>
> Romans 8:17–19, 22–23

When we stand before the bema seat of Christ, we will be rewarded for the suffering we have endured in his name. At that moment, our pain, grief, loneliness, and any vestige of sadness will disappear, swallowed up by the glory of God.

When you suffer emotionally—when you are lonely, afraid, depressed, or shy—the Lord can be an anchor in the midst of a sea of unhappiness. But you cannot enjoy his help unless you draw close to him.

When you suffer loss—the loss of a job, a friend, or a loved one—the Lord will comfort you and provide your needs. He knows you better than you know yourself, and he is familiar with the abyss of grief. Isaiah knew that Jesus would be "despised and rejected by men, a man of sorrows, and familiar with suffering. Like one from whom men hide their faces he was despised, and we esteemed him not" (Isaiah 53:3).

You may be suffering spiritually. Though most people don't like to admit their doubts, you may experience days when your soul feels as dry as a desert and God seems millions of miles away. You may be angry at God; you may feel he no longer cares for you.

When those dark times come, know this: God is strong enough to handle your questions and your riotous emotions. He knows your frame; he knows even the intricate workings of your mind. And he is with you, even in the arid sand of the desert places.

CHAPTER 5

THE INCORRUPTIBLE CROWN

Everyone who competes in the games goes into strict train-
ing. They do it to get a crown that will not last; but we do
it to get a crown that will last forever.

1 Corinthians 9:25

We know there will be many rewards in heaven, but Scripture specifically names five stephanos crowns for special
service—the incorruptible crown, the crown of rejoicing, the
crown of life, the crown of righteousness, and the crown of glory.
I am thrilled to know that these crowns are available to all of us—
if our deeds on earth qualify us for the reward.

The Crown That Cannot Tarnish

Before we can be rewarded for doing works that glorify God,
we'd better learn how to stop doing the sinful things that dishonor our Lord.

The King James Version of 1 Corinthians 9:25 uses the word
incorruptible to describe the crown given to those who learn how
to master the old, sinful nature. Describing this crown, using the

images of a race and a boxing match, Paul continues, "Therefore I do not run like a man running aimlessly; I do not fight like a man beating the air" (9:26 NIV).

If you have ever tried to stick to a diet, you know how hard it is to master your appetite. I had to lose some extra pounds after the birth of my last baby, and there were days when I wondered if I could conquer my desire for more food than I needed!

When we become Christians, we are forgiven from sin and assured a home in heaven, but as long as we live in these physical bodies we will have to wrestle with the sinful nature that still resides within us. It is a tough battle, and nobody knew that better than the apostle Paul. As he wrote in Romans, "I know that nothing good lives in me, that is, in my sinful nature. For I have the desire to do what is good, but I cannot carry it out. For what I do is not the good I want to do; no, the evil I do not want to do—this I keep on doing. Now if I do what I do not want to do, it is no longer I who do it, but it is sin living in me that does it" (7:18–20).

How, then, do we master this desire to do the sinful things we don't want to do? Paul has the answer: "Therefore do not let sin reign in your mortal body so that you obey its evil desires. Do not offer the parts of your body to sin, as instruments of wickedness, but rather offer yourselves to God, as those who have been brought from death to life; and offer the parts of your body to him as instruments of righteousness" (Romans 6:12–13).

It sounds so simple. If we want to defeat sin, we should offer our bodies to God. On another occasion, Paul said we should consider ourselves "living sacrifices" (Romans 12:1). But short of climbing on an altar and lying prostrate all day, how does one actually accomplish this?

I can give you the answer in one word: *discipline*.

How Do I Discipline Myself?

Paul was not only a gifted apostle, he was also a great writer. He compared our struggle to overcome sin and earn the incorruptible crown to competing in a physical contest. It's an appropriate metaphor, for you can't expect a woman who has spent all her life sitting in an easy chair in front of the TV to jump up and run a marathon or compete on a balance beam. World-class athletic competition requires world-class training. Dedicated athletes rise before the sun to practice and train; watch every bite they eat; and obtain the help of coaches, trainers, and other experts who can help them learn how to achieve peak performance.

In the same way, you can't expect a Christian woman who has spent her entire life sitting in a church pew to go out and withstand strong temptation; conquer all her bad habits; and spread peace, love, and joy to everyone she knows. World-class Christian living requires world-class spiritual training. Christians who live victorious lives practice spiritual disciplines; watch their appetites; and enlist the help of pastors, teachers, and wise counselors who can help them defeat sin and live in victory.

Unfortunately, not many churches today stress spiritual disciplines, yet they are as important to achieving victory over sin as learning scales is to a budding concert pianist.

In his delightful book *The Life You've Always Wanted,* John Ortberg writes that a disciplined person is "someone who can do the right thing at the right time in the right way with the right spirit." Ortberg further explains that a disciplined follower of Jesus is *not* someone who creates rigid rules and adheres to them, but rather someone "who discerns when laughter, gentleness, silence, healing words, or prophetic indignation is called for, and offers it promptly, effectively, and lovingly."[1] I love that definition!

My coauthor, Angela Hunt, once had the opportunity to interview Dr. Dallas Willard, author of *The Spirit of the Disciplines.* Dr. Willard defined spiritual disciplines as an activity you choose to engage in so you'll be able to do what you cannot do by direct effort.

> In other words, the spiritual discipline is not essentially different from any kind of discipline. The person who practices the piano could not sit down and play—by direct effort—a Beethoven sonata the way it should be played. But through hours of practice, a pianist does what he can do in order to do what he can't do. That's the basic idea of a discipline.[2]

A spiritual discipline differs from the discipline required by a musician or athlete, however, because in spiritual disciplines, we prepare ourselves to interact with God, his Spirit, and his Son. We prepare ourselves to receive grace and strength we would not otherwise be able to receive.

"The purpose of every spiritual discipline," says Jan Winebrenner in *Intimate Faith: A Woman's Guide to the Spiritual Disciplines,* "is to train us to relate to God, to abide in him, and to discover his sufficiency in all things."[3]

Let's look to Scripture for an example of a spiritual discipline. Remember Jesus' encounter with James, John, and Peter in the Garden of Gethsemane? Jesus took these three disciples to the garden and asked them to pray with him. When he returned a short while later, he found all three men asleep. He said, "Could you men not keep watch with me for one hour? Watch and pray so that you will not fall into temptation. The spirit is willing, but the body is weak" (Matthew 26:40–41).

The disciples were willing to pray with Jesus, but they lacked the discipline to see the matter through. That same night, before the garden encounter, Peter had promised Jesus that he would never fall away. Jesus assured Peter that he would. "I tell you the truth," Jesus said, "this very night, before the rooster crows, you will disown me three times" (Matthew 26:34).

Years later, however, Peter would be more disciplined—even to the point of dying before denying his Lord.

Train with Eternal Rewards in Mind

If we want the Lord Jesus to give us the incorruptible crown, we need to train like an Olympic athlete. Instead of running and jumping and stretching, however, we can practice spiritual disciplines such as prayer, meditation, solitude, fasting, study, simplicity, submission, service, confession, worship, guidance, and celebration. The practice of spiritual disciplines helps us grow strong enough to resist temptation and defeat human weaknesses. If we never train ourselves in spiritual matters, we may remain baby Christians who wilt in the winds of temptation and adversity.

In her book *To Heaven and Back,* Rita Bennett notes the work involved when we strive to win the incorruptible crown. "It takes endurance, discipline, and commitment to be an Olympian. Should we as followers of Jesus be careless in our life's witness for him before the world and powers of darkness? We can't be perfect . . . but if we fall down, we can pick ourselves up, wash off, and get back into the race."[4]

Without the practice of spiritual disciplines, a Christian remains ineffectual and incompetent. Dallas Willard explains: "If you were to ask a pianist why practice is important, he'd tell you that without it he couldn't perform. I was astonished years ago to learn that a concert pianist practices between four and seven hours a day. Of course, that explains why most people aren't concert pianists."[5]

Dr. Willard's comments about training reminded me of my own training for the Miss America pageant. I danced ballet to "Via Dolorosa"—a song that lasted a mere one hundred and fifty *seconds*. But to perfect my ballet, I had to train two or three hours a day, five days a week, for two entire *years*. I won the Miss America talent competition, but I wouldn't have been successful if I hadn't trained until my feet were aching.

"Wait a minute," you may be saying, "I've been a Christian for years and have never heard of spiritual disciplines. Are you telling me about something new?"

Not really. You may have learned about spiritual disciplines and not realized what you were learning. There are many spiritual disciplines, but in studying the life of Christ we can pick out several that Jesus practiced: fasting, solitude, meditation, sacrifice, silence, study, simplicity, prayer, submission, and service.

You are probably already familiar with prayer and study. You have undoubtedly heard about fasting and service. But how long has it been since you spent a predetermined amount of time practicing any of the above disciplines?

I know, time is precious. We have obligations to our family, our work, our homes, and our friends. But we also have an obligation to Christ, and if we exercise wisdom (seeing things from God's eternal perspective), we will begin to understand that having a new car in the garage is not nearly as important as winning rewards in heaven.

How I Learned the Value of Discipline

In the previous chapter, I told you about my emotional struggle to adjust to my cochlear implant. It was a difficult time for me, and at the peak of my struggle I wondered if I was doing anything worthwhile as a mother, a wife, or a Christian.

But during this time, as God softly spoke encouragement to my heart, I began to look for practical solutions to some of my bothersome problems. Dr. Niparko, who implanted my cochlear device at Johns Hopkins hospital, had suggested that I spend one hour alone every day reading and listening to books on tape. The only time I could do this was 6 a.m., before my boys awoke. But I resisted doing so, because I needed time alone with God.

I found the answer in a CD recording of the Bible, allowing me to listen to the Word as I read along. But at first it was anything but easy. I read and listened to the first psalm about fifteen times and could only understand one word: *psalm*. The sounds distracted my reading, and I became completely discouraged.

Then I remembered one of my favorite quotes. The founder of *Ebony* magazine, John Johnson, once said that great dreams were too far away for us to reach, but with each small step we can grow closer to accomplishing our great dreams. I could take small steps, couldn't I? I could begin to practice a discipline.

At this point God showed me that he made two ears for a reason, and he expected me to use both. So I grabbed my hearing aid and used both the cochlear implant and my hearing aid as I listened to the Bible CD. With that technique, I made progress—and continued in my disciplined effort.

My heart lightened and filled with hope in God. One day I was talking on the phone to my father, who has a raspy voice. I have never been able to completely understand him with my hearing aid, so we haven't talked much on the phone.

We had talked for about twenty minutes when it hit me— we were *talking!* And I hadn't had to call John over to help me understand what Dad was saying!

As I progressed, my heart filled with even more joy. My boys' sadness went away, and I grew calmer even when they were tired and fussy. I was happy when John came home from work. And through it all, I felt Jesus' love surrounding me.

The daily discipline of listening to God's Word did more than train my ears—it also trained my heart.

Establish Your Priorities

So how do you practice spiritual disciplines in the routine of daily life? First, set aside a block of time. Decide that growing spiritually stronger is important to you, and resolve to pay the price. Some Christians are content to pass through life without growing, and they will stand before the bema seat in embarrassed silence when the incorruptible crowns are awarded. If you want to win this crown, you can make a conscious decision to become more like Jesus with every passing day.

When you say, "I don't have time," what you're really saying is "I don't value this above all the other things in my life." You are saying, in effect, that you place your family, your business, your hobbies, and your home above the things that would help you be more like the Savior.

If you are willing to commit yourself to the practice of spiritual disciplines, you can begin tomorrow. But Dallas Willard suggests that before you begin, you pick up your Bible and a highlighter. Read through the Gospels and mark the things Jesus actually *did,* not the things he said. By doing this, you will see Jesus as a student, as a son who took care of his mother. You will see that he frequently withdrew from others to spend the night in prayer. His disciplines—solitude, silence, meditation, prayer, service, and study—are the things you can practice first.

"Spiritual disciplines are not commands, but counsels," Willard notes. "Clearly Jesus assumed that we would fast and that we would go into our closets and pray. In the biblical world everyone practiced spiritual disciplines, even the pagan religions. I don't think anyone can succeed at following Christ without them."[6]

Willard also points out that our spiritual forefathers frequently practiced spiritual disciplines: Jesus, Paul, Martin Luther, John Calvin, John Wesley, and others. And although the Bible does not expressly say, "Thou shalt practice spiritual disciplines," it does say "train yourself to be godly" (1 Timothy 4:7). Spiritual disciplines are the exercises by which we train ourselves to grow in faith, grace, and obedience.

After you have highlighted Jesus' actions in the Gospels, pray about what the Lord would have you do. The idea is not that you should spend a month alone in a mountain cabin, but that you learn to be led by the Spirit. He will lead you to do things you could not do by direct effort.

How do you decide which disciplines to practice first? Dallas Willard says we should practice the disciplines that answer our weaknesses:

> People are different, and every person will have to make that decision. There is no formula or list which fits all cases; the life of discipline should be one undertaken in a line of guidance from Jesus, through his Spirit, about our personal lives.
>
> Also, a life of discipline is one that is undertaken experimentally. You learn as you go, you expect to fail, and to learn from your mistakes. For example, a day in solitude and silence will be a great learning experience for most people and probably what they expect will not be what happens. They have to learn how to be silent, how to be alone with God.[7]

In her book *A Closer Walk,* Catherine Marshall describes the time she felt God asking her to "fast" for twenty-four hours from being critical of others.[8] Perhaps God has spoken to you about a critical spirit—or a defeated attitude. A spiritual fast may be what you need to break a destructive habit.

You're Not Training Alone

If you begin to be spiritually disciplined, God promises to meet you: "You will seek me and find me when you seek me with all your heart" (Jeremiah 29:13). You will grow stronger, and God will gain a fit vessel to use in his service. If you want to be a tool for the kingdom of God, if you really want him to use you, spiritual disciplines will help you become a spiritual powerhouse.

If you had an urgent need, who would you call to ask for prayer? Most of us know at least one or two people whom we consider to be "prayer warriors." They seem to have an inside line to heaven; they pray fervently, and their prayers are answered. How do you think they became prayer warriors? Prayer is not a special gift; it is a discipline. Prayer warriors become strong prayers because they pray often, they pray for concentrated periods of time, and they pray fervently. They have trained in the discipline of prayer.

Prayer warriors can help you in your time of need. They can serve as your mentors, your friends, your accountability partners. All of us who are following Christ are in training for the prize, so why shouldn't we train together?

All Discipline Is Difficult At First

Suppose you clear your calendar, unplug the television, and decide to spend the day alone with God in silence. What will likely happen?

You may think you are going to go out of your mind. If you're like most people, you have been so busy running here and there that it feels strange to sit and seek peace. You may feel guilty and uncomfortable; you may be nagged by the sensation that you're forgetting something important.

It takes discipline to sit in a chair and tune in to the still, small voice of God.

A friend of mine told me about a time she was a speaker for a Christian conference. The retreat center was very nice, with hotel-type rooms, but the guest rooms had no television, no radio, no telephones. When my friend retired to her room after a full day of speaking, the silence nearly drove her batty! "I don't usually watch much TV at night, and I had a book to help pass the time," she told me. "But I'm used to the background noise. That room was just too quiet!"

Yet quiet is what we need if we want to concentrate on hearing the voice of God. I'm sure there are many times when God speaks, but we are too distracted by the sounds of this noisy world to hear him.

In a strange way, I have been used to silence, which allowed me not to be easily distracted by noises as I spent quiet time with God. Before receiving my cochlear implant, I used to imagine heavenly classical music and pictured myself dancing for God above the clouds. But now that I hear better, I can get frustrated by hearing new and strange sounds as I'm reading and listening to the Word. One day while listening to Bible verses on CD, I became aware of a strange sound coming from the yard. I took off my headphones, looked outside, and discovered that I was hearing our new pet. When I brought the baby chick home, I had thought he was a black hen. But clearly we owned a proud rooster.

I have learned something over the past few months: God was wise not to give me my hearing when I used to beg him for it. During those younger years, because I couldn't hear, I spent more time listening to his heavenly music in my heart.

For beginners, spiritual disciplines can be grueling. You may set aside an hour for prayer, so you curl up in your chair and begin to pray. Halfway down your list of prayer requests you might feel guilty that you're not doing something, and it won't occur to you that you *are* doing something. The time spent in meditation, prayer, study, and silence is a spiritual investment that will result in eternal rewards. One of the hardest things for over-programmed contemporary Christians is to sit and be still.

Could you manage an hour of fervent praying? Could you meditate on a passage of Scripture for a morning? Could you sit alone by a lake for an entire afternoon?

We are all different; what is easy for one will be difficult for another. But the point of discipline is to draw on God's strength, to listen to his voice, to enjoy being with him even in our solitude. If you are sitting by the lake alone, God is there too. Is he enough?

Always.[9]

CHAPTER 6

THE CROWN
OF REJOICING

*For what is our hope, our joy, or the crown in which we
will glory in the presence of our Lord Jesus when he comes?
Is it not you?*

1 Thessalonians 2:19

I once heard a story about a man who worked out a special deal
with God. He wanted to be able to bring one suitcase with him
to heaven. At last the Christian found himself standing in a heavenly chamber before the throne of Christ. Before the angels began
to replay his deeds, one of them pointed to the suitcase in his
hand. "What's that?"

The man clutched the suitcase to his chest. "The Lord said
I could bring it."

The angel shrugged. "Okay, but let's see what's inside."

The man opened the suitcase, and the angel peered into it.
The suitcase was lined with bars of solid gold.

"Lord," the angel called, looking toward the throne of God.
"Why'd you give this guy permission to bring in paving material?"

Ah . . . so many of the things we hold dear are worthless in the Kingdom of God.

That story is not an accurate representation, of course, because we can't take material possessions to heaven. We can, however, work to see that lost souls join us there and contribute to our soul winner's crown. This is usually called the *crown of rejoicing,* as that is the term used in the King James Version of 1 Thessalonians 2:19.

Let me introduce you to an amazing British man who strongly influenced life in the American colonies because he lived for two things: the glory of God and the salvation of souls.

Whitefield's Passion

On a cold November evening in Philadelphia, more than six thousand people filled the streets surrounding the courthouse. The year was 1739, and the crowd had gathered to hear a young preacher, George Whitefield. Without the benefit of notes or a microphone, Whitefield stood and preached a message of salvation, not hesitating to explain the gospel so it made sense intellectually and emotionally.

Within a few months, Philadelphia was transformed. Benjamin Franklin, a local resident, wrote, "From being thoughtless or indifferent about religion, it seemed as if all the world were growing religious, so that one could not walk through the town in an evening without hearing psalms sung in different families of every street."[1]

Without benefit of television or radio, Whitefield spoke to millions of Americans during his ministry, preaching more than eighteen thousand sermons in the colonies alone. He preached to aristocrats and commoners and held services for slaves. Although some people criticized him for supporting the institution of slavery, Whitefield was one of the few ministers who believed and proclaimed that slaves had souls. He warned slave owners that if they did not allow their slaves to learn about salvation, they were putting themselves in danger of the wrath of God.[2]

Even those of us who are not called to be preacher-evangelists can emulate the character of George Whitefield. Those who knew him admired his qualities, particularly his burning love for Jesus and his self-denial. Whitefield often practiced spiritual disciplines, including prayer, fasting, and moderation in eating and drinking. He frequently spent entire nights in Bible study and devotion. He cared little for money, choosing instead to live a frugal life of simplicity. When he died, he left no fortune behind, but oh, what riches he sent on to heaven—not bars of gold but saved souls.

You are probably familiar with evangelists who hold citywide meetings, but in Whitefield's day such events were rare. Biographer J. C. Ryle writes that Whitefield was "the first to see that Christ's ministers must do the work of fishermen. They must not wait for souls to come to them, but must go after souls, and 'compel them to come in.'"[3] Ryle of course is using the same metaphor as Jesus, who called his disciples by saying, "Come, be my disciples, and I will show you how to fish for people!" (Matthew 4:19 NLT).

One of Whitefield's favorite expressions was "Let the name of George Whitefield perish so long as Christ is exalted." And yet I put the name of George Whitefield before you because through his life we are able to learn more about the crown reserved for soul winners. As J. C. Ryle noted, Whitefield was one of the first in his generation to realize that we cannot wait for people to come to us. If we honestly want to win souls, we must be willing to take the gospel out of the church.

Courage to Reach Out

Far too many Christians have become happily cocooned in the world of Christian culture. Christians today enjoy a broad and profitable counterculture—we have Christian books, Christian films and videos, even Christian yellow pages. We listen to Christian music, hang Christian art in our homes, and read Christian novels on the beach. We can send our children to Christian schools, have them play on Christian sports leagues, and send them to Christian colleges.

All of those things are fine and good—but have we become so involved in pursuing all things Christian that we have forgotten about reaching the world?

The crown of rejoicing is reserved for soul winners, yet the temptation is strong to ignore the lost souls around us. Sometimes we are too intimidated to speak up for Christ; sometimes we assume someone else will do it. There are times when our society seems to practice tolerance for everyone *but* Christians, and when we encounter hostile attitudes we want to shrink into our shells like frightened tortoises.

I remember how lonely I felt when I was in high school. Being a Christian teenager at a public high school is not easy, especially where you have been told that it is not proper to bring a Bible to school or to pray publicly before class or in the cafeteria. It seemed easier to do bad things than to do spiritual things; every once in a while, I would see students smoking pot or drinking beer in the restrooms. Often I would see couples making out in the halls— not exactly an appropriate activity for school. I saw teachers who were not willing to intervene when students were making bad decisions; perhaps they were afraid of being sued or fired.

Over time, I felt left out. Having low self-esteem, I was not verbal about my faith. And I saw other Christian classmates who chose to be quiet. But I desperately wanted to say something about my love for Jesus, so when I signed up to compete in the Junior Miss program, I chose Twila Paris's song "How Beautiful" for my ballet.

When I won the talent competition, God sparked a fire in my heart to talk about my faith. It was as if he said, "You see? I blessed your willingness to witness through your dance. I can bless your willingness to witness through your words too."

Not long after that competition, I asked my prom date to help me keep my promise to Jesus about keeping my body pure for my future husband. He agreed to do that and we had a great time. The following year, I not only danced to the same song in the Miss Alabama Pageant, but I also began to tell the media, judges, and my fellow contestants about Jesus.

I think the Holy Spirit was beginning to prepare me for the crown of rejoicing back then, and he continues to guide me today.

The Call of Love

"The fruit of the righteous is a tree of life, and he who wins souls is wise" (Proverbs 11:30). I see great wisdom in the soul-winning philosophy of Fanny Crosby—a blind nineteenth-century poet who wrote lyrics to more than nine thousand gospel songs, including "Blessed Assurance," "He Hideth My Soul," "I Am Thine, O Lord," "Near the Cross," "Pass Me Not," "Redeemed," "Rescue the Perishing," and "To God Be the Glory." Her songs themselves nudged countless people toward and into the kingdom, but she took an even more active role in soul winning.

Fanny Crosby often visited missions and homeless shelters and sat among lice-covered men to demonstrate the love of Christ. She did not believe in pointing out other people's faults, but tried to show the love of God.

"Don't tell a man he is a sinner," she said. "You can't save a man by telling him of his sins. He knows them already. Tell him there is pardon and love waiting for him. Win his confidence and make him understand that you believe in him, and never give up."[4]

When competing for the Miss Alabama title, I learned that a fellow pageant contestant was a faithful Christian who wanted to become a missionary. She told me about a conversation she'd had with an alcoholic. This man said he was too drunk for God to accept him. She answered, "Drinking beer will not take you to hell. Not accepting Jesus will take you to hell. He loves you and wants to take you to heaven."

The man's eyes filled with tears as he said, "No one has ever told me how much Jesus loves me."

That night, another soul reserved a place in heaven.

Winning Souls Begins at Home

God wants our concern for souls to include those in our own household. Paul wrote, "Fathers, do not exasperate your children;

instead, bring them up in the training and instruction of the Lord" (Ephesians 6:4).

The most important thing we parents can do in our roles as spiritual leaders is teach our children about Jesus. Involving your children in church attendance is important, but don't assume they will learn everything they can know about God through Sunday school or Christian videos. They can hear you talking about God in a natural way; they can see how you depend on him and think about him every day, in every situation. The old maxim is true: Important life lessons are more often caught than taught.

Several years ago Dr. Clyde Narramore, a pioneer in the field of Christian psychology, said that one of the best ways parents can love their children is by leading them to the Lord at an early age.

> It doesn't take an awful lot of maturity to realize that you've done things that are wrong, that sin displeases God, and that God sent Jesus Christ to die for us. Children can use computers at three and four. They can know and do much by the time they are five. Consequently, they can understand the gospel at a very young age.
>
> I think it may be detrimental to a person's intellect if he has to live in this world and not understand many basic concepts such as sin, salvation, Christian growth, and God's working throughout the world.[5]

My boys are still very young, but even at this age there are days when I wonder if I'll be able to be the godly mother they need. Sometimes I feel I am raising my children more through trial-and-error than by God's principles! What works with one child does not necessarily work with another, and what works when they are two will not work when they are fifteen.

Still, God promises to supply all my needs and to provide wisdom, and I know I can depend on him to keep his promises. He will give me what I need, when I need it. As Philippians 4:19 tells us, "My God will meet all your needs according to his glorious riches in Christ Jesus."

My husband, John, and I are doing our best to be sure that our sons hear Bible stories and see that we live the lessons those stories teach. We believe building a Christian home is the most important thing we can do for our children.

Every night since our boys were born, John and I take time to sing "Jesus Loves Me" and say a prayer before we leave their room. Not long ago, my boys spent the weekend with my mother-in-law. The next morning, she called me.

"Little John came into my room this morning," she said, "and wanted to know why I didn't sing 'Jesus Loves Me' and say a prayer last night."

That night, she followed our bedtime routine—and she loved it.

I also take the time to read a children's devotional book before my boys take their naps in the afternoon. We also take them to Sunday school and play Christian music in the car. And when my boys come up and find me reading the Bible, I know I'm setting a good example—something I hope they'll remember for a long, long time.

The Harvest

If you want to be an effective soul winner, sometimes you will have to sacrifice your own personal rights and privileges. The apostle Paul, who was born a free citizen of Rome and had been highly educated, learned to humble himself and surrender his own rights in order to win souls to Jesus. He wrote, "Though I am free and belong to no man, I make myself a slave to everyone, to win as many as possible" (1 Corinthians 9:19).

Not only will those who spread the gospel receive the crown of rejoicing, but they will experience rich joy on earth! The Bible often compares soul winning with farming; some people till the soil, some sow the seed, some reap. And all share in the joy of a successful harvest! "He who goes out weeping, carrying seed to sow, will return with songs of joy, carrying sheaves with him" (Psalm 126:6).

Do not be discouraged if you share the gospel and the person you are trying to reach does not immediately respond. You have sown the seed, and that's important.

A friend of mine once planted a garden in his backyard. "I realized something," he said, "when I went to get a tomato that wasn't quite ready. When you try to pluck a fruit that isn't ripe, you'll have to bend and twist and possibly even break the stem. But if you wait until the fruit is ripe, with just one little tug the fruit falls into your hand."

That is a powerful metaphor for soul winners. You see, we don't save people. Jesus is the only Savior; his Spirit the only one who convicts. If you present the gospel simply and clearly, you don't have to pull and tug and twist at someone else's heartstrings. If the person is ready, the fruit will fall into your hand.

No Greater Rejoicing

Jesus said, "Even now the reaper draws his wages, even now he harvests the crop for eternal life, so that the sower and the reaper may be glad together" (John 4:36).

I don't know if you have ever had the pleasure of leading a person to Christ, but there is nothing quite like the joy of knowing that someone who was lost has been found. Someone without hope has gained the Prince of Peace, and someone once destined for an eternity apart from God has reserved a mansion in heaven.

When I was a college freshman, I pledged a sorority. I had been assigned a "big sister" who was supposed to look after me. But I kept telling her that something was missing in this sorority, and I wasn't feeling good about the first fraternity party we were supposed to attend.

Despite my misgivings, I went—and found that everyone present was drinking and making out, activities that made me uncomfortable. I asked my big sister to take me back to the dorm, so she did.

Later I joined a Christian group, and my heart filled with joy. I wanted to leave the sorority, but my big sister encouraged me to stay. When she asked why I wanted to leave, I tried to explain and then asked her to go with me to one of the campus Bible study groups.

She did and fell in love with Jesus.

I did not preach to her. I simply tried to follow the Lord's leading in my life, and she watched me closely.

Six years later, I was honored to see how the Lord has worked in her life. She's a missionary on a college campus in the Southeast. She has planted seeds of love in many students' hearts. I have been so blessed to see how she has grown in her love for Jesus.

"Remember this," wrote James, "Whoever turns a sinner from the error of his way will save him from death and cover over a multitude of sins" (5:20).

There is no joy quite like the joy that comes from soul winning. The only emotion that comes close is the thrill parents feel when their children are born. We rejoice when we greet our little ones for the first time, but when a soul enters the Kingdom of God, the entire body of Christ and all the angels rejoice too!

Jesus described the experience in a story:

> Suppose a woman has ten silver coins and loses one. Does she not light a lamp, sweep the house and search carefully until she finds it? And when she finds it, she calls her friends and neighbors together and says, 'Rejoice with me; I have found my lost coin.' In the same way, I tell you, there is rejoicing in the presence of the angels of God over one sinner who repents.
>
> Luke 15:8–10

Whether you are the sower or the reaper, when you share your faith in Christ, you are reserving a Crown of Rejoicing at the bema seat.

And there's more: "Those who lead many to righteousness [will shine] like the stars for ever and ever" (Daniel 12:3).

CHAPTER 7

The Crown
of Life

*Blessed is the man who perseveres under trial, because when
he has stood the test,
he will receive the crown of life that God has promised to
those who love him.*

James 1:12

On Friday, October 6, 1536, the crowd parted silently as the gates of the prison yawned open. The prisoner who climbed into the cart paused for a moment, indicating that his jailer should take the letter protruding from an opening in his tunic. The jailer took the letter, and the prisoner nodded, satisfied.

The condemned man climbed into the cart, knelt in the straw, and nearly lost his balance as the donkey leaned into the traces. They crossed a stone bridge over the River Senne and halted just outside the fortifications of the castle in Brussels. The cart progressed slowly, hampered by the throng that had gathered by the roadside.

The prisoner's jailers were grateful for the mob. They hoped to make an example of this man who had violated the emperor's decree and wanted the townspeople to witness the punishment of a heretic.

The crowd instead witnessed the victory of a martyr. William Tyndale, charged with violating the imperial decree that forbade anyone to teach that faith in Christ alone justifies men and women before God, died without recanting his faith or his convictions.

The calm prisoner was led to the stake. While the executioner fastened him to the post, Tyndale yelled, "Lord, open the king of England's eyes!"

Those were his last words. Immediately afterward he was strangled, then flames were lit to consume his body. But though men on earth could destroy his flesh, they could not touch his soul—or his eternal reward. I am certain that at the bema seat Jesus will reward William Tyndale with the crown of life.

This wonderful reward is bestowed on those who endure trials for Christ's sake: "Do not be afraid of what you are about to suffer," Jesus said. "I tell you, the devil will put some of you in prison to test you, and you will suffer persecution . . . Be faithful, even to the point of death, and I will give you the crown of life" (Revelation 2:10).

Incredible Sacrifice, Immeasurable Results

William Tyndale encountered opposition from nearly everyone when he insisted that common people needed to be able to read the Bible in their common language. Born in England in the latter part of the fifteenth century, he received his master's degree from the University of Oxford, then was ordained and continued studies at Cambridge. There he practiced spiritual disciplines, particularly the discipline of study. In *Fox's Book of Martyrs,* the author notes that Tyndale was "fully ripened in the knowledge of God's word."

At this point he began to translate the New Testament from Greek into English, so uneducated people could learn to read it for themselves, instead of relying on increasingly corrupt ecclesiastical officials.

Tyndale talked about his goal of publishing his translation. When a prominent clergyman protested, Tyndale replied, "If God spare my life, ere many years I will cause a boy that driveth the plow to know more of the Scriptures than thou dost."[1]

Tyndale printed his English version of the New Testament in 1525. In the next decade he translated the first fourteen books of the Old Testament from Hebrew to English.[2]

Eventually Tyndale was betrayed by a friend and arrested. He refused an advocate and a lawyer, choosing to serve as his own defense. While in prison at the castle, he continually talked about Jesus to his guards. His witness, faith, and steadfastness were so strong that during the eighteen months of his confinement, he led his jailer, the jailer's daughter, and other relatives to faith in Christ.

And if you have a King James Bible in your home, you owe much to William Tyndale. Despite those who criticized him and said his Bible was full of heresy—"pestilent glosses"—he wrote, "I call God to record against the day we shall appear before our Lord Jesus that I never altered one syllable of God's word against my conscience, nor would do this day, if all that is in earth, whether it be honor, pleasure, or riches, might be given me."

One historian notes, "Tyndale is the man who taught England how to read and showed Shakespeare how to write. No English writer—not even Shakespeare—has reached so many."[3]

Tyndale was opposed, but he did not back down. Tyndale was persecuted, but he did not waver in his conviction. Tyndale was mocked and scorned and taken to court, but he did not lose faith in the Word of God. Tyndale was killed, but his work—and his testimony—remains.

Jesus said, "Do not be afraid of those who kill the body but cannot kill the soul. Rather, be afraid of the One who can destroy both soul and body in hell" (Matthew 10:28).

Like you and me, William Tyndale will one day stand before the Lord Jesus. We will all rejoice when we see him receive a well-earned crown of life.

But he will not be the only one to receive it. We will also rejoice with millions of believers over the centuries, and even now from China, Cuba, Afghanistan, Pakistan, and other nations, who have endured trials for Jesus' sake.

A Costly Faith

We Americans have been so blessed: Few of us suffer for our faith like Christians in other countries. In the United States we do not worry about being awakened in the night by secret police or taken away from our loved ones because we profess faith in Christ. Our churches do not have to meet in secret, and children can carry their Bibles to school if they choose.

Yet in some countries, churches must meet secretly; families are often torn apart as government authorities send family members to prison camps; Christians are even being persecuted to the death.

By visiting www.persecution.org, you can find up-to-date reports on Christians suffering persecution in China, India, Iraq, Sudan, Vietnam, Indonesia, Sri Lanka, Uzbekistan, and many other countries. Christians have been cruelly murdered in African nations, imprisoned in China, and attacked in India. Missionaries have been forced to flee many countries because the work of spreading the gospel has proven to be too dangerous.

A 2002 U.S. State Department Report names several nations that engage in widespread repression of religion—particularly Christianity. In China, the report says, "unapproved religious and spiritual groups remained under scrutiny and, in some cases, harsh repression."[4]

Citizens in Cuba who worship in officially sanctioned churches are often subjected to surveillance by state security forces. In Myanmar, the government views religious freedom as a threat to national unity. The Laotian government inhibits religious practice by all religions, particularly Christianity, that fall outside mainstream Buddhism. Members of underground churches in North Korea have been beaten and arrested, and some have been killed. Christians in Vietnamese churches have been forced to recant their faith or face severe consequences.

Persecution is not a new phenomenon. Satan has always hated the gospel of Jesus Christ, for it frees people from the tyranny of sin. Satan's agents have always opposed the work of Christ. Persecution arose around Jesus himself and caused great havoc in the early days of the church. Stephen was the first Christian martyr named in the Bible (and, interestingly enough, his name means *crown*), but you can be sure millions of others have followed since the day Stephen looked toward heaven and died. Between 1400 and 1557, more than one thousand people were burned for the sake of the gospel.[5] Church researcher David Barrett claims that in 1994 some 156,000 Christians worldwide surrendered their lives for Jesus.[6] In sacrificing their very lives, they will receive their reward—a crown of life—when they stand before the bema seat.

Standing Firm

You don't have to be martyred to receive the crown of life. The Bible says anyone who withstands the test of trial is a candidate for this reward.

In her book *Sacred Stories,* Ruth Tucker relates a telling account of a day in the life of Christina Matson, an itinerant missionary in the early 1900s. Speaking in Orrock, Minnesota, to a schoolhouse full of people, she suddenly heard breaking glass. Through two smashed windows the platform and congregation was barraged with ripe and rotten eggs.

An eye witness reported, "The first egg smashed on Miss Matson's head . . . She was preaching with the Lord's prayer as her subject, and significantly had come to the very sentence 'forgive us our trespasses as we forgive those who trespass against us,' when the enemy struck."[7]

This story reminds me that persecution does not always happen in some faraway land, where Christianity is being introduced. It can happen here, and in ways that may not be life threatening but nevertheless call for courage.

Perhaps some of you know this form of persecution firsthand. You may be persecuted by unbelieving family members; perhaps you are mocked or teased or even ostracized because of your belief in Christ. Your family may have cut you off when you became a follower of Christ; you may have been lied about and hurt by your loved ones.

But Jesus will reward you for standing firm. As he stood to teach the lessons we call the Sermon on the Mount, Jesus said, "Blessed are you when people insult you, persecute you and falsely say all kinds of evil against you because of me. Rejoice and be glad, because great is your reward in heaven, for in the same way they persecuted the prophets who were before you" (Matthew 5:11–12).

You may not suffer persecution for the cause of Christ, but I believe the Lord will also judge us for what we did to help those who are suffering persecution. We can help our brothers and sisters who are undergoing trials. We can spread the word of their condition, we can pray, and we can support those who are working to promote religious freedom in other countries.

And when this earthly life is over, we will cross eternity's threshold and find ourselves in the presence of the Lord. We will live eternally in supernatural bodies, and we will wear the crown of *life*—full, abundant, and eternal.

I love the way George Duffield expressed this thought in a poem that has become an old standby hymn. Duffield wrote the lines in 1858 to memorialize the dying words of a clergyman colleague in Philadelphia: "Tell my brethren of the ministry, wherever you meet them, to stand up for Jesus."[8]

Stand up, stand up for Jesus, the strife will not be long,
This day, the noise of battle, the next, the victor's song.
To him that overcometh, a crown of life shall be;
He with the King of Glory shall reign eternally!

CHAPTER 8

THE CROWN OF GLORY

Be shepherds of God's flock that is under your care, serving as overseers—not because you must, but because you are willing, as God wants you to be; not greedy for money, but eager to serve; not lording it over those entrusted to you, but being examples to the flock. And when the Chief Shepherd appears, you will receive the crown of glory that will never fade away.

1 Peter 5:2–4

It is not for us to decide who will receive rewards at the bema seat, but I can just imagine the long line of teachers, preachers, disciples, and prophets who will receive the crown of glory, which will be given to spiritual shepherds. The faithful minister of a small church, the flamboyant evangelist who taught millions via television. Youth pastors; ministers of music; missionaries; American public school teachers who did not shy away from presenting a God-centered view of history, language, and art; grandmothers who faithfully taught two-year-olds in Sunday school—all of these people are candidates for the crown of glory.

Here in this chapter I'd like to introduce you to a few whom I see as excellent examples.

A Servant-Leader Who Helped Changed a Nation

As a very young girl, Amy Carmichael and her mother visited a tea shop in Belfast, Ireland. When Amy got home, she could not forget a ragged little girl she had seen outside the window, peering in at—and longing for—the delicious pastries. Amy sat down by the fire and wrote a poem:

> When I grow up and money have,
> I know what I will do.
> I'll build a great big lovely place
> For little girls like you.

Amy Carmichael kept her promise, although she admitted later that for a time she forgot all about it. "But," she wrote, "there is One who remembers even a child's promises. And though the little girls who were to come to the 'great big lovely place' were not to be the least like that little girl, yet they were in need, far greater need than she was. And the wonderful thought of our Father was far, far greater than mine. He had sons as well as daughters in His heart that day."[1]

Amy Carmichael, who built a home of refuge for children in Dohnavur, India, was instrumental in leading thousands from that country into the loving fold of the Chief Shepherd. At the time of her death in 1951, nearly a thousand children were living in the Dohnavur family, including 120 older boys and girls in training as teachers or nurses or studying in Christian schools.

The eldest of seven children, Amy was born in 1867 in a sea-coast village in what is now Northern Ireland. As an adult she would remember a number of lessons learned as a child. At three years of age, she prayed passionately, "God please give me blue eyes." After this prayer of simple faith, Amy looked in the mirror, saw her brown eyes, and realized that "no is an answer" as well as yes.

She also remembered a conversation she had as a teen with an older widower who said, "You must never let yourself think, 'I have won that soul for Christ.'" He illustrated his point with the story of a man who asked a stonebreaker, "Friend, which blow broke the stone?"

The stonebreaker replied, "The first one and the last one, and every one between."

Armed with humility and perseverance, Amy grew increasingly committed to serving the Lord and sharing the gospel with those living in darkness. As she wrote to her mother, "The longing to go to them, and tell them of Jesus, has been strong upon me . . ."

When an opportunity opened, Amy went to Japan. She lived there only a few months but picked up concepts that influenced her future work. One day when visiting a dying Japanese woman, she presented the gospel through an interpreter. Right at the potential moment of decision for Christ, the woman grew distracted by Amy's English gloves. Noticing this, Amy returned home, took off her clothes, donned a kimono, and vowed never again to risk so much for so little.

Because of her ill health, no doctor would allow her to serve in China, Japan, or the tropics. Instead, she went to South India in November 1895 and never left. In India, she saw why God gave her brown eyes. Having this physical feature in common with the Indian people made it easier for her to minister to them. She often wore an Indian dress and stained her arms and hands with coffee to visit places off limits to foreign women. Blue eyes would have immediately aroused suspicion.

In 1901 a frantic seven-year-old girl called Pearl Eyes came to Amy, begging for help, claiming she had escaped from a temple. Upon investigation, Amy learned that the girl was one of many young temple prostitutes—girls sold to the temple staff and groomed to satisfy men who worshiped there. Amy discovered that children, especially those who were handsome or intelligent, were never "unwanted"; they could be sold for a tempting price.

With this new knowledge, Amy had a new mission to seek and save children destined for temple service. Sometimes she could convince mothers to place the children in her care. Other times she resorted to purchasing children from greedy parents who would sell them to the highest bidder.

Pearl Eyes was the first of many young girls welcomed into Amy's home. In time she was even given babies born to temple prostitutes. Recognizing the severe needs of these homeless, helpless children, Amy established the Dohnavur Fellowship, a sprawling complex that at one time housed more than a thousand members of Amy's "family."

Biographer Nancy Robbins notes that Amy occasionally felt the sting of criticism from other missionaries. "You are just a nursemaid now," they said. "Not a real missionary at all. How can it be right for you to stop teaching the village women about the Lord Jesus and to spend all your time giving bottles to babies?"[2]

But Amy thought of the Chief Shepherd Jesus, who was not too proud to wash his disciples' feet, and she realized her efforts would count for the future. If God allowed her to bring up her children as faithful servants of Jesus Christ, writes Robbins, "they would be able to do far more for Him in their beloved India than she, a foreigner, could ever do."[3]

In 1931 Amy prayed, "Do anything, Lord, what will fit me to serve Thee and help my beloveds." That afternoon she slipped into a pit and suffered a debilitating injury. For the next twenty years she lived in confinement; she described her new capacity as "keeping of the charge." From her room, Amy wrote thirteen books, revised previous books, and penned thousands of letters to family, friends, and her many children. A steady stream of people flowed to and from her bedside. Over the door hung a sign, "The Room of Peace." Even in her weakness, Amy was the center of Dohnavur; her room was a shelter in the time of storm.

In 1948 temple prostitution was officially outlawed in India, but poverty, neglect, and abandonment still caused hundreds of children to need a loving home. Even today Amy's Donhavur work continues, staffed by Indian doctors, nurses, dentists, and housemothers.[4]

Model Leadership

Amy's story inspires me on two counts. I see her loving perseverance. Not all of us are given the opportunity to lead others, but when we are given this responsibility, we must fulfill it with all diligence. Even if you are given responsibility only for a small committee at church, you can take that responsibility seriously, as if you are working for the Lord himself. If you help in the youth department, with the bed babies, or with the senior saints, learn to see each person in your care as someone for whom the Lord Jesus gave his life.

The apostle Paul said, "For I have not hesitated to proclaim to you the whole will of God. Keep watch over yourselves and all the flock of which the Holy Spirit has made you overseers. Be shepherds of the church of God, which he bought with his own blood" (Acts 20:27–28).

I'm also inspired by Amy's story of the stonecutter—knowing the importance of humility in leadership. We need to keep the example of Jesus before us. For though he was God incarnate, possessing all power, he did not come to earth to demand homage, but to pour out his life as a sacrifice for those he came to save. He said, "Just as the Son of Man did not come to be served, but to serve, and to give his life as a ransom for many" (Matthew 20:28).

Jesus' servant leadership is best illustrated in John's account of the Last Supper (13:3–17), in which Jesus dramatically washed and dried his disciples' feet. You or I might be startled if we went to a dinner and someone brought out a bowl to wash our feet, but the practice was not unusual in biblical times. Men and women traveled on dusty roads in sandals. By the end of the day, people's feet were hot, tired, and excessively sandy. The ritual of foot-washing was a soothing and welcome evening respite.

Trouble is, servants were usually assigned to the bowl and towel. The host of the dinner *never* washed anyone's feet. Imagine how startled the disciples were when their Lord and Master took off his tunic, picked up the bowl, and knelt to unstrap their dirty sandals. John relates the conversation between Jesus and Peter:

"No," said Peter, "you shall never wash my feet."

Jesus answered, "Unless I wash you, you have no part with me."

"Then, Lord," Simon Peter replied, "not just my feet but my hands and my head as well!"

Impetuous Peter! At first he is indignant that his Lord should have to wash his feet; then Jesus explains that if Peter doesn't get the big picture, he's out of the picture.

"Okay, Lord," Peter says. "Then count me in for the entire bath!"

When Jesus had finished washing their feet, he asked, "Do you understand what I have done for you?"

> You call me 'Teacher' and 'Lord,' and rightly so, for that is what I am. Now that I, your Lord and Teacher, have washed your feet, you also should wash one another's feet. I have set you an example that you should do as I have done for you. I tell you the truth, no servant is greater than his master, nor is a messenger greater than the one who sent him. Now that you know these things, you will be blessed if you do them.
>
> John 13:13–17

On another occasion Jesus said, "The greatest among you will be your servant. For whoever exalts himself will be humbled, and whoever humbles himself will be exalted" (Matthew 23:11–12).

I am convinced that some of the best-known preachers will stand before the judgment seat of Christ and not receive the crown of glory because they received their rewards of applause and praise while on earth. But there will be others who receive the crown, having been leaders in more untraditional ways.

Learning to Serve While Leading

The crown of glory is not reserved for ordained ministers or missionaries—almost every Christian has, at one time or another, been granted authority over others. Harold Willmington writes, "This leadership role may have been that of a parent, pastor, teacher, employer, etc."[5]

In 1946, Truett Cathy and his brother Ben sold a car, cleaned out their savings accounts, and took out a bank loan. With the resulting $10,600, Ben and Truett opened a restaurant in the Atlanta suburb of Hapeville. With only ten counter stools and four tables, the place was so small the brothers named it the Dwarf Grill.

As the years passed, Truett Cathy experimented with ways to prepare chicken. In 1967, he opened the first Chick-fil-A at Atlanta's Greenbriar Mall and pioneered the concept of fast food within a mall setting. Today there are more than one thousand Chick-fil-A restaurants around the world.

Why am I mentioning a chicken restaurant in a chapter on those who lead the body of Christ? Because Truett Cathy has demonstrated servant-leadership not only in the church, but in the business world. He is a devout Christian who built his life on hard work, kindness, compassion, and biblical principles. Without exception, his restaurants are closed on Sundays. He is a dedicated philanthropist, directing a Chick-fil-A program that has awarded more than $14.6 million in scholarships to Chick-fil-A employees and establishing a foster care program that gives a good home to more than 120 children. "I play the part of grandpa for those children," he says. "It is a great deal to drive up to the house and hear the kids yelling, 'Grandpa is here!'"

Cathy told an interviewer that one of the keys to his success was the ability to keep his priorities properly ordered. "You may be successful in business," he said, "but if you fail in other areas of life and in relationships with your family, friends, or with the Lord, then no manner of business can make up for that. Thus we must never lose sight of what is important."[6]

As a businessman and church man, Cathy, I trust, will receive his crown of glory. I also see a crown awaiting people like Hazel James who have quietly invested their hearts, lives, and time in the lives of those they served in Christ's name.

Hazel's Shepherd Service

My coauthor, Angela Hunt, has told me about Hazel James. If you had met Hazel, who is with the Lord now but lived in Largo, Florida, from a distance you would have noticed her wheelchair or the way her hands curled into rigid arcs in her lap. But when you got up close, you would have noticed her wide, honest eyes and her bright smile.

As a teenager Hazel developed rheumatoid arthritis, which causes inflammation of tissues in and around joints and may affect nearly all the body systems. For Hazel, rheumatoid arthritis was a steadily disabling disease, but in the midst of suffering Hazel found joy, not in what she could do for herself, but in what she could do for others.

Hazel always said that she reached the pinnacle of personal fulfillment at a time when most people would hang their heads in discouragement. "When I first got in a wheelchair, I wanted to do something for God," she told Angela. At the point of her greatest physical disability, Hazel found an opportunity to shepherd young lives, working with Mission Friends, a program at her church for four- and five-year-olds. "So many people just sit back and don't do anything," she said. "They say they are Christians, but they don't do God's work. But working with kids is a great joy. I treat them like they're my kids."

In addition to teaching with Mission Friends, Hazel spent two mornings each week serving as cashier for her church's thrift shop and was active in a singles' telephone ministry, a prison Bible study, and nursing-home visitation. "I can't give a lot of money to God's work," she said, "but I can do the best job I can at things that glorify God by serving others."

Hazel lived in constant pain, but before she died, she left a message for others in similar situations: "I read in the paper about a man who felt he couldn't do anything because he was disabled. He wanted permission to die from the courts . . . I wanted so badly to write him and tell him not to give up. It doesn't matter what's wrong with you—if you have God on your side, you can do anything."

Hazel may not have realized it at the time, but hundreds of men, women, and children in her sphere of influence were grateful that she was willing to shepherd so many. She understood what Paul wrote in 2 Corinthians 4:16–18. Though he doesn't refer to a crown, he does mention a reward of "glory":

Therefore we do not lose heart. Though outwardly we are wasting away, yet inwardly we are being renewed day by day. For our light and momentary troubles are achieving for us an eternal glory that far outweighs them all. So we fix our eyes not on what is seen, but on what is unseen. For what is seen is temporary, but what is unseen is eternal.

Some servants never receive earthly fame or riches, but a crown of heavenly glory awaits them—isn't that an amazing thought?

CHAPTER 9

THE CROWN OF RIGHTEOUSNESS

I have fought the good fight, I have finished the race, I have kept the faith. Now there is in store for me the crown of righteousness, which the Lord, the righteous Judge, will award to me on that day—and not only to me, but also to all who have longed for his appearing.

2 Timothy 4:8

I love watching the years go by. The years seem to pass faster these days, but I don't mind getting older. Each passing year reminds me that the earth is one year closer to the year when Jesus will come again. That event is known as the rapture.

You won't find the word *rapture* in the Bible, but you won't find the word *God* in the book of Esther either, and the divine fingerprint is all over that story. The rapture is described many times in Scripture, and there's a reward reserved for those who look forward to this event: the crown of righteousness.

This crown is one of the easiest to talk about and the most difficult to put into practice! We all love to talk about the Lord's return. On difficult days we are quick to say, "Lord, come quickly!"

But do you really live each day as if it could be your last? Do you act and think and spend your money as if heaven is your real home and earth only a temporary stopping place?

Before we delve into how the Lord's coming relates to our present lives, let's look at the Scripture that explains the rapture most clearly. Paul wants believers to know that they don't have to worry about those who die before the Lord's return:

> For the Lord himself will come down from heaven, with a loud command, with the voice of the archangel and with the trumpet call of God, and the dead in Christ will rise first. After that, we who are still alive and are left will be caught up together with them in the clouds to meet the Lord in the air. And so we will be with the Lord forever. Therefore encourage each other with these words.
>
> 1 Thessalonians 4:16–18

Notice that we will meet the Lord Jesus "in the air"—this is not the Second Coming, when Jesus literally sets foot on the Mount of Olives. This is a separate event that precedes the Second Coming. This is the ingathering of all who follow Christ, all the believers who have accepted him in what is commonly called "the church age."

When Will the Rapture Take Place?

People have been predicting the appearance of Jesus for ages, and with every passing year these predictions grow more numerous and more certain. But Jesus said,

> No one knows about that day or hour, not even the angels in heaven, nor the Son, but only the Father. Be on guard!

Be alert! You do not know when that time will come. It's like a man going away: He leaves his house and puts his servants in charge, each with his assigned task, and tells the one at the door to keep watch.

Therefore keep watch because you do not know when the owner of the house will come back—whether in the evening, or at midnight, or when the rooster crows, or at dawn. If he comes suddenly, do not let him find you sleeping. What I say to you, I say to everyone: "Watch!"

Mark 13:32–37

Theologians hold differing views about when the rapture could occur, but I believe Jesus could summon his church at any moment. Many people ridicule the idea of all Christians suddenly vanishing from the earth, but the Bible says such cynics are actually a sign that we have entered the last days and his coming is near!

First of all, you must understand that in the last days scoffers will come, scoffing and following their own evil desires. They will say, "Where is this 'coming' he promised? Ever since our fathers died, everything goes on as it has since the beginning of creation."

2 Peter 3:3–4

How will the rapture unfold? Quickly! The moment Jesus appears in the air, a trumpet will sound and we will be instantly caught up to be with him. No matter where you are or what you were doing, you will find yourself with Jesus. And because these earthly bodies aren't designed for subsonic atmospheric flight, we will be changed—our bodies will become supernatural, glorified, and strong! Christians who have died will be instantaneously raised in supernatural bodies as well, and together we will meet the Lord in the air!

Paul explains it this way:

> Listen, I tell you a mystery: We will not all sleep, but we will all be changed—in a flash, in the twinkling of an eye, at the last trumpet. For the trumpet will sound, the dead will be raised imperishable, and we will be changed. For the perishable must clothe itself with the imperishable, and the mortal with immortality. When the perishable has been clothed with the imperishable, and the mortal with immortality, then the saying that is written will come true: "Death has been swallowed up in victory."
>
> 1 Corinthians 15:51–54

Living with the Lord's Coming in Mind

We know that the Lord is coming. Once he comes, we will stand before the judgment seat of Christ. Our earthly lives will be done. There will be no going back to finish projects, right wrongs, or dispose of earthly treasures.

Once the trumpet sounds, our earthly deeds are finished. Knowing this, how should we live day to day? The crown of rejoicing is given to those who long for Christ's appearing—so how should we live while longing for the Lord?

John and I first began dating while I was traveling as Miss America. I met him and liked him, and as we grew closer I began to long for the days when I would see him again. My Miss America schedule was hectic. I was jetting all over the country, while John was living and working in Washington, D.C.

Now I am grateful for the time we spent apart, like the old adage about absence making hearts grow fonder. Because I didn't see John every day, I couldn't take his affection for granted. Spending time with him was a real treat.

I still travel (though my schedule is not nearly as busy as in my Miss America days), and there are times when I'm on a plane and find myself longing for home. I want to see the faces of my beloved boys; I want to fall into my husband's arms and just stand there, letting him take the burden from my weary heart.

I think that's the feeling God rewards with the crown of righteousness. He gives it to those who yearn for heaven and for the moment when they can look upon the Savior's face. In her book *The Homesick Heart,* Jean Fleming notes, "Redemption is the great theme of the Bible, and homesickness seeps from the pores of every page."[1]

Because I long for home when I'm away, I have learned to live within certain boundaries while I'm on the road. I try to stay rested and healthy, so I'll be in good shape when I come home to my children. When I'm on the road, I don't flirt with other men, because I want my husband to know he can trust me to be faithful. I do my work to the best of my ability when I'm traveling and speaking, but I'm always thinking about the end of the road—and home.

In the same way, living with the rapture in mind means we see our time on earth in a different light. Joni Eareckson Tada wrote a whole book about anticipating heaven. But, she notes,

Don't think such heavenly mindedness makes us pilgrims no earthly good. Don't pooh-pooh it as looking at the world through pie-in-the-sky, rose-colored glasses. Sojourners who think the most of the next world are usually those who are doing the highest good in this one. It is the person whose mind is only on earthly things who, when it comes to earth, does little good.[2]

We do our work as best we can, but we look forward to going home. We don't flirt with the world's affections, because we want our hearts to remain devoted to Jesus. We guard our energy and our health so we can better serve our heavenly king.

Most of all, we see our time away from our eternal home as temporary. We realize that the treasures we have accumulated on earth will mean nothing once we join Christ in the heavens. Our bank accounts will be inaccessible; our earthly homes will be out of reach. Our clothing, our cars, all the things we cherished will be useless and meaningless.

The only things that matter are the things we invested in the Kingdom of God.

Focus on the End

Any swimmer, runner, or plowman will tell you that if you want to move ahead in a straight line, you must set your sights on something at the end of the line and move steadily toward it. The swimmer, runner, or plowman who looks to the left and right as she moves ahead will end up creating a wavy line!

In the same way, the Lord promises that if we eagerly look for his coming, we will not be distracted by the petty concerns of this world. If we are focusing on the Kingdom of God, we won't be so worried and upset by the things that happen in this life. And our perspective—which will be strikingly different from that of the people around us—will be a powerful testimony for the truth of the gospel.

I am trying my best to live each day with an ear cocked for the sound of the trumpet—for Jesus is coming again. And Jesus "is the jewel at the center of all that is taught about the final things."[3]

This old gospel song titled "The Meeting in the Air" expresses my desire for Christ's return. It ends by quoting the eager ending of the Bible, Revelation 22:20, but it also introduces the topic of my next chapter—meeting Christ, the bridegroom—and you and me, the heavenly bride.

> O the hope of his appearing—
> How it lights the dreary way.
> How it girds our souls with courage
> For the "little while" we stay!
> For it cannot be much longer
> Till the Bridegroom calls us home;
> Surely, surely he comes quickly!
> Even so, Lord Jesus, come!
>
> A. A. P.

CHAPTER 10

THE LAMB'S BEAUTIFUL BRIDE

O bride of Christ, rejoice;
Exultant raise thy voice
To hail the day of glory
Foretold in sacred story.
Hosanna, praise, and glory!
Our King, we bow before thee.
Then go thy Lord to meet,
Strew palm-leaves at his feet,
Thy garments spread before him
And honor and adore him.
Hosanna, praise, and glory!
Our king, we bow before thee.[1]

The judgment seat of Christ will be a time of celebration for all Christians who have served Christ faithfully, sent treasures on ahead, shared the gospel, withstood temptation and the pull of the flesh, and suffered for the sake of the gospel. Our works—the good things we have done—will be richly rewarded.

Does it seem strange to talk about works this way? We are so often taught that we are saved through faith, not through works, that often we forget that works are important too. Our work does nothing to save us—only Christ can do that—but they are the deeds we do in order to please our heavenly father. Like the children we are, we do our best to glorify and thank him.

The apostle John, after receiving a visit from an angel who showed him glimpses of the future, wrote, "Then I heard a voice from heaven say, 'Write: Blessed are the dead who die in the Lord from now on.' 'Yes,' says the Spirit, 'they will rest from their labor, for their deeds will follow them'" (Revelation 14:13).

After you and I have stood before Christ's judgment seat and witnessed the review of our words, deeds, and attitudes, the Judge of all the earth will move to recognize our rewards or our losses.

The things we have done well—for Christ's glory—will merit reward. Paul wrote,

> If any man builds on this foundation using gold, silver, costly stones, wood, hay or straw, his work will be shown for what it is, because the Day will bring it to light. It will be revealed with fire, and the fire will test the quality of each man's work. If what he has built survives, he will receive his reward. If it is burned up, he will suffer loss; he himself will be saved, but only as one escaping through the flames.
>
> 1 Corinthians 3:12–15

Harold Willmington points out that of the six categories mentioned in this portion of Scripture, three (gold, silver, and precious stones) are things that survive and thrive in fire. Wood, hay, and straw, however, will be totally consumed by flame.[2]

Can you imagine the sight? I don't know if the fire Paul speaks of is literal or metaphorical, but I understand the principle involved. Let's say I visited a nursing home on two different occasions. The time I visited to show Christ's love to the residents will survive the testing fire as a brilliant diamond; the time I visited to impress a friend with my good works will be burned up as crackling straw.

The times I patiently taught my children about God will come through the purifying flames like silver; the times I hurried through their bedtime Bible stories may vanish in smoke.

The day I took the time to speak words of mercy and wisdom to my neighbor will be a sparkling emerald; the day I passed on a piece of gossip disguised as a prayer request will only add fuel to the fire.

The money I happily gave to missions will result in a brilliant ruby; the money I grudgingly gave to the church building program will burn like dry paper.

The things I did for myself will vanish; the things I did for Christ will remain. They will find their way into my hope chest.

I believe that once we are saved by grace, our salvation is assured. But because we can lose our rewards, we must be careful that we aren't distracted by temptation or dissuaded from doing God's will. Hold fast to what is right and listen for the Spirit's leading. If we continue in doing good for Christ, if we persevere in suffering and train ourselves through spiritual disciplines, we will be rewarded with crowns, precious adornments, and spotless gowns of fine linen!

The Hope Chest

Let me recommend to you Randy Alcorn's wonderful little book, *The Treasure Principle.* Read it and you are in for a life-changing experience! Alcorn quotes a Scripture that is familiar to most of us: "Do not store up for yourselves treasures on earth, where moth and rust destroy, and where thieves break in and steal" (Matthew 6:19). What we often fail to see, however, is the promise contained in the next verse: "But store up for yourselves treasures in heaven, where moth and rust do not destroy, and where thieves do not break in and steal. For where your treasure is, there your heart will be also" (Matthew 6:20–21).

Do you recognize the promise? While you can't take your earthly possessions with you to heaven, you can send treasures on ahead! Jesus *told* us to store up treasures in heaven by investing our earthly goods in heavenly treasures. He understood that when we focus on the eternal instead of the temporary, our focus lines up with God's.

Jesus will reward us for investing our treasures in heaven. He told the rich young ruler, "If you want to be perfect, go, sell your possessions and give to the poor, and you will have treasure in heaven" (Matthew 19:21).

Randy Alcorn says, "Our instinct is to give to those who will give us something in return. But Jesus told us to give to 'the poor, the crippled, the lame, the blind . . . Although they cannot repay you, you will be repaid at the resurrection of the righteous' (Luke 14:12–14). If we give to those who can't reward us, Christ guarantees he will personally reward us in heaven."[3]

One of the ways we can lay up treasures in heaven is by filling our heavenly hope chests. Throughout the ages, young women who have just become engaged usually prepare for their marriage by collecting the things they will need in their new home. I don't know if you had one, but Angela Hunt tells me she had a complete set of pots and pans in hers by the time she was fifteen years old!

I had never heard of a hope chest until Angela told me about hers. I didn't collect pots or pans or quilts. I was always taught to get a college education and a job because career should come before marriage. My family has been hurt by divorce, you see, and I don't remember hearing good things about marriage from anyone except one of my aunts. So for me, career came first. I didn't even know how to cook when I married John! Sometimes I wish I'd had a little training in the arts that would help me be a good wife and mother.

What can Christians do to prepare for their marriage to Christ? We won't need material things in our heavenly home because Jesus has met all our needs. He'll give us supernatural bodies that can handle the demands of an eternal existence. He'll give us the bread of life and living water. We'll walk on streets of gold and pass through gates of pearl ... I can get a little dazzled just thinking about the beauty of heaven!

So if we can't bring anything material into heaven, what can we bring? The Bible is very specific on this matter—the things we bring to the marriage—the items we put in our "hope chest"—are the righteous acts we do to glorify God. If we want to come well-prepared to the marriage of the Lamb of God, it is time to start thinking about how we will prepare for the big day.

The Wedding of the Lamb

The Bible frequently uses a specific metaphor to describe the coming reunion of Christ and his church. (We'll look at a few of these verses in chapter 11.) To better understand all the aspects of this rich symbolism, let's first review the chain of events in a traditional biblical wedding.

In Old Testament times, the bridegroom or a representative of the groom's father went out in search of a bride. Think of Abraham's servant finding Isaac's wife, Rebekah. Young women might agree to the marriage without ever seeing their future husbands, as Rebekah consented to her marriage before meeting Isaac.

After the bride's father and the groom's representative agreed to the union, they settled on a bride price—maybe a pair of camels or a group of silver bracelets. The Hebrew word for this agreed-upon price is *mohar.* A scribe drew up a contract of marriage, the *ketubah,* recording the bride price and the groom's promises to honor, support, and live with her. From the moment of agreement, the bride and groom were legally married even though they did not yet live together. At the conclusion of the betrothal ceremony, the couple shared a cup of wine, then the groom or his representative took his leave, promising to prepare a home for his bride before he returned for her.[4]

How does this Jewish tradition translate to the image of Jesus as the bridegroom of the church?

Christians are the bride of Christ, sought by the Holy Spirit and purchased with a bride-price of the life-blood of sinless Jesus. "Do you not know that your body is a temple of the Holy Spirit, who is in you, whom you have received from God? You are not your own; you were bought at a price. Therefore honor God with your body" (1 Corinthians 6:19–20).

As the bridegroom, Jesus prepares a home for us. He told his followers, "In my Father's house are many rooms; if it were not so, I would have told you. I am going there to prepare a place for you. And if I go and prepare a place for you, I will come back and take you to be with me that you also may be where I am" (John 14:2–3).

We have already received wedding gifts. When we accepted Jesus, God gave us eternal life! The Holy Spirit has given us love, joy, peace, longsuffering, kindness, goodness, faithfulness, gentleness, and self-control.

Our betrothal contract is the Word of God, for it contains all the promises our loving groom has made on our behalf.[5]

When I became engaged, I only had about six months to prepare for my marriage to John. I'm so glad I have an entire lifetime to prepare for my wedding to Jesus! I became a follower of Christ when I was fifteen years old, so now I've had almost fifteen years to grow in love for my Savior. Through my dance, worship, Bible study, and prayers, I am preparing myself for the coming marriage between Christ and his church.

The Fetching of the Bride

The second part of a biblical wedding took place some time after the groom had prepared a home for his bride. When the new house met his father's approval, the groom journeyed to the bride's home, picked up his betrothed, and carried her to their new home where friends had gathered for a festive wedding supper.

At some point in the celebration, the bride would slip away to put on the special garments she had prepared for the wedding. If she was a wise bride, she had prepared a beautiful garment. She would dress in her prepared wedding clothes, then step out to be presented to the groom's father and meet all his friends in their new home.

The church is still waiting for this second part of our heavenly wedding to commence. One day the Father will tell Jesus the time has come to summon his bride. We will rise through the air to meet Jesus in the clouds.

Nothing will go wrong with this wedding. The groom will not be late. The bride will not be frazzled. No one will protest when the groom takes his bride's hand. We will stand before Christ as holy and pure people, redeemed through his precious blood and adorned with the righteous acts we have performed in his name and for his glory.

In Ephesians 5:27, Paul referred to this metaphor, saying that Christ gave himself for his bride "to present her to himself as a radiant church, without stain or wrinkle or any other blemish, but holy and blameless."

I remember taking great care to select the perfect wedding gown when I married John. I tried on forty different gowns before narrowing the choice down to three. Everyone I asked liked all three, but I finally chose the one that would make me look most like a southern belle because I'm from Alabama and was about to marry a southern man. I wanted a dress that would make me look beautiful and that would make John proud. I hoped a mere glimpse of me walking down the aisle would take his breath away!

As I wanted to please my earthly husband, so I want to please my heavenly groom. Once I leave this earth and join Jesus in heaven, I want to be attired in the most stunning wedding clothes.

Wait a minute, you may be thinking. *What wedding clothes are you talking about?*

The garments are described in Revelation 19:7–8: "Let us rejoice and be glad and give him glory! For the wedding of the Lamb has come, and his bride has made herself ready. Fine linen, bright and clean, was given her to wear. (Fine linen stands for the righteous acts of the saints.)"

J. Vernon McGee notes, "Through the ages believers have been performing righteous acts which have been accumulating to adorn the wedding gown. By the way, what are you doing to adorn that wedding gown?"[6]

Our wedding garment and its decorations will be the righteous deeds that survived the testing fire when we stand before the judgment seat of Christ. Perhaps the diamonds, rubies, emeralds, gold, and silver—which represent the things we did to glorify Christ—will adorn our spotless linen garments as we step out to join our heavenly groom at the wedding feast. Perhaps we will be wearing our crowns. I don't know exactly how this will happen or what it will look like, but I understand the principle behind the metaphor: *The works we have done will determine how well prepared we are when we meet Jesus.*

Will you have a glittering wedding garment when you greet the Savior?

Esther Held Onto Her Faith—and Her Crown

The story of Esther, a beautiful Jewish girl who became queen of the Persian Empire, is one of my favorite Old Testament accounts. I'm sure there wasn't a safer person in Persia on the day she was crowned—after all, she and the king had garrisons to protect them. But the king's right-hand man, Haman, secretly hated the Jews and didn't know his new queen was Jewish. When he convinced the king, through deception and trickery, to sign a death warrant for all the Jews in Persia, not even the king knew he had signed an execution decree for his own queen!

Esther would have lost her life, but she bravely stepped forward and acted to save herself and her people. It's important that you understand a little of the background story: Esther's predecessor, Queen Vashti, had been sent into exile for disobeying a direct order of the king.

When Esther learned of the death warrant, she knew she had to speak to the king, but a Persian law decreed instant death for anyone who approached the king uninvited. An interloper was spared only by the king's special pardon.

When Esther dressed in her finest gown to address the king, she had been fasting and praying for three days (practicing spiritual disciplines!). She had to be physically weak, as well as frightened. If she failed today, she would die on the spot and her people would soon be murdered.

As she approached the throne, the guards drew their swords. Esther caught her breath; the king looked at her—and lifted his scepter.

In the end, the Jews survived, and Esther remained safe in the palace.

Faced with a seemingly insurmountable problem, Esther could have thrown up her hands and wept in despair, but she chose to place her faith in God. She became the instrument God used to preserve her people, and by doing so, she held fast to her crown. As Dennis Jernigan says, "Trust in [God] not only brings *him* glory, it becomes *my* glory! As I crown him the one I trust with my life, he crowns me with all he is."[7]

That crown was probably the last thing on Esther's mind as she walked on shaky legs into the king's presence. She was thinking about her people, about God, about the king's love. She was praying to find acceptance and approval in his eyes.

That's what we'll find when we stand before our heavenly bridegroom arrayed in our glorious crowns and fine white linen.

Jesus Is My Heavenly Groom

Several years ago, I wrote a poem about being the bride of Jesus. I love this image, because whenever things go wrong, I know I will always be beautiful and adored in the eyes of my heavenly bridegroom.

As I wander at the beach,
You surprise me with your sparkling water like a diamond,
With breezes on my face,
You unveil my hair with your strong, yet gentle hands.
The seagulls ring the bells with their voices,
And the waves applaud as you say, "Arise, my love and come with me."
Then night falls, as the stars play the harps for your romance,
The moon lights a candle in your chamber.
The breeze smoothes my face, bringing your fragrance.
You draw me into your mysterious, yet loving spirit.
The diamond still sparkles

But no longer can hold your overflowing love.
As the diamond spills more onto the sand,
Your heart shines through my body onto little miracles.
Suddenly I remember where I came from.
Here I lie down in your beautiful chamber as a bride
Who does not wish to go back to her world.
I look up at the gentle stars,
Thinking this will not last longer.
Your kiss fills my heart with sweet wine.
Then the warm waves rub my feet,
Encouraging me to look down.
There you show me how beautiful a bride I am in your eyes.
And as the stars sparkle on my head,
You crown me with your praise and everlasting life.
I am the bride of the mighty King of all kings.

CHAPTER 11

CROWN HIM WITH MANY CROWNS!

Crown him with many crowns,
The Lamb upon his throne;
Hark! How the heavenly anthem drowns
All music but its own!
Awake, my soul, and sing
Of him who died for thee;
And hail him as thy matchless King
Through all eternity.

Matthew Bridges

When I was a child, the length of time between Christmases seemed an eternity. As I have grown older, time passes more quickly. And my elders tell me that soon I'll look around and wonder where the length of my lifetime went.

How I wish we could realize that the here-and-now that holds us so firmly in its grip will one day seem like a distant memory. Compared to the eternity we'll spend in heaven, this life is only a brief "boot camp" in which we learn how to be like Jesus.

As we move through our days and weeks, let's remember that our purpose is not to amass possessions or to make a name for ourselves in a world that is as temporary as a sunset. Our purpose is to glorify God, and that purpose will not change when we enter eternity. But, as I have written throughout these pages, between earth and heaven there is a "checkpoint"—a moment when the Lord will evaluate how well we have fulfilled our destiny during the short time we spent on earth.

When we stand before the bema seat, our works, which are a reflection of our hearts, will tell the Lord how prepared we are to rule and reign with him in God's Kingdom. Before we set about that work, however, we can anticipate not a coronation, not a pageant, not a parade, but a *wedding!*

The Most Spectacular Wedding Ever

The Bible is filled with stories about weddings. The first wedding was Adam and Eve, when God presented them to each other and blessed their union. God loves seeing men and women come together and Scripture is sprinkled with love stories: Isaac and Rebekah, Rachel and Jacob, Ruth and Boaz.

Jesus chose a wedding as the occasion to perform his first miracle, turning water into wine. And many of Jesus' parables were stories of bridegrooms and weddings—pictures of the most beautiful union in the world, the marriage for which we and our forefathers have longed:

"The kingdom of heaven is like a king who prepared a wedding banquet for his son" (Matthew 22:2).

"At that time the kingdom of heaven will be like ten virgins who took their lamps and went out to meet the bridegroom" (Matthew 25:1).

"Be dressed ready for service and keep your lamps burning, like men waiting for their master to return from a wedding banquet, so that when he comes and knocks they can immediately open the door for him" (Luke 12:35–36).

The wedding of the ages is coming, and every passing day brings it closer! Scripture gives us many details about this future wedding, including information on all the wedding participants.

The *host* is none other than God the Father, who has sent out his servants to invite guests and prepared his Son to receive a bride. He is the one who tells the groom when it is time to fetch the bride; he is the one to whom the sought-after bride will be presented in all her glorious finery. "A certain man was preparing a great banquet and invited many guests. At the time of the banquet he sent his servant to tell those who had been invited, 'Come, for everything is now ready'" (Luke 14:16–17).

As I discussed in chapter 10, the *bridegroom* is Jesus, the Son who paid the bride-price and is preparing a place for us. John the Baptist alluded to the coming wedding and Jesus' status as the bridegroom. He told his disciples that he was not the anticipated Messiah, but the forerunner, more like a groomsman: "The bride belongs to the bridegroom. The friend who attends the bridegroom waits and listens for him, and is full of joy when he hears the bridegroom's voice. That joy is mine, and it is now complete" (John 3:29).

Jesus called himself the bridegroom. When people asked him why his disciples did not mourn and fast like the disciples of John the Baptist, he replied, "Can you make the guests of the bridegroom fast while he is with them? But the time will come when the bridegroom will be taken from them; in those days they will fast" (Luke 5:34–35).

And who is the *bride?* Anyone who has accepted Christ's gift of salvation is part of the bride of Christ. To a group of believers Paul wrote: "I am jealous for you with a godly jealousy. I promised you to one husband, to Christ, so that I might present you as a pure virgin to him" (2 Corinthians 11:2).

In a longer passage Paul compares the relationship between husbands and wives to the mysterious relationship between Christ and his beloved bride, the church.

> Wives, submit to your husbands as to the Lord. For the husband is the head of the wife as Christ is the head of the church, his body, of which he is the Savior . . .
>
> Husbands, love your wives, just as Christ loved the church and gave himself up for her to make her holy . . .
>
> This is a profound mystery—but I am talking about Christ and the church.
>
> Ephesians 5:22, 23, 25, and 32

If Jesus is the groom, the church the bride, and God the host, who are the *guests* at this magnificent wedding? John gives us a clue when the angel commanded him to write, "Blessed are those who are invited to the wedding supper of the Lamb!" (Revelation 19:9).

Harold Willmington believes the guests include all believing Gentiles who were converted prior to the coming of the Holy Spirit at Pentecost or after the rapture of the church and also descendants of Abraham who have accepted Jesus as their messiah.

In her book *To Heaven and Back,* Rita Bennett notes, "The whole company of heaven comes to the feast of the ages . . . The Jewish wedding feast has its biggest banquet after the wedding and the seven-day honeymoon. It is likely that our Messiah will follow this pattern. This will be the greatest banquet ever known."[1]

Unlike American society, where the bride is expected to be the belle of the ball, this wedding reception is designed to honor the groom for having chosen such a beautiful bride.

Of the wedding feast, John Hagee writes, "Jesus will be honored, not because of what we are, but because of what He has made us."[2]

At some point—I don't know exactly when—we will look upon our Lord and Savior with tears in our eyes. We who are clothed in fine linens and precious jewels are not worthy of the honors he has allowed us to wear.

We will cast our crowns before Jesus, knowing that he alone is worthy of praise.

Casting Our Crowns Before Him

I'd like to change the scene for a moment and take you to the throne room of heaven as John described it in Revelation 4. Jesus, the Lamb of God, is seated on the throne. He is surrounded by the lights of precious stones, and the blinding light of glory hurts our eyes as we behold his brightness. Angels surround the throne, worshiping and adoring the one who sits on it, and around the angels are twenty-four seats occupied by twenty-four elders—representatives of the church—in white robes. Each of the elders is wearing a crown of gold.

Then, John says,

> The twenty-four elders fall down before him who sits on the throne, and worship him who lives for ever and ever.

They lay their crowns before the throne and say: "You are worthy, our Lord and God, to receive glory and honor and power, for you created all things, and by your will they were created and have their being."

Revelation 4:10–11

J. Vernon McGee says the "crowns of the church are laid at Jesus' feet as an act of submission and worship. Many people talk of there being a crown for them over there. Frankly, if we get a crown at all, I think that after we wear it for a while and the newness wears off, we are going to feel embarrassed. What in the world are we doing wearing a crown? The only One worthy up there is the Lord Jesus."[3]

When we cast our crowns at Jesus' feet, we make it clear that our crowns are not and could never be something in which we can take pride. If we had done these righteous acts to promote ourselves, we would never have earned the crowns in the first place.

No, our crowns are temporary possessions, beautiful adornments the Lord allows his bride to wear as we enter the marriage supper. They are intended to reflect *his* glory, not ours.

Dwight Pentecost notes that the act of placing our crowns at Jesus' feet is one way by which we will glorify Christ, and this destiny—to glorify God—will continue forever. Because "reward" is scripturally associated with brightness and shining (see Daniel 12:3; Matthew 13:43; 1 Corinthians 15:40–41, 49), our heavenly reward may be an eternal "capacity" to glorify Christ.

The greater the reward, the greater the bestowed capacity to bring glory to God. Thus in the exercise of the reward of the believer, it will be Christ and not the believer who is glorified by the reward. Capacities to radiate the glory will differ, but there will be no personal sense of lack in that each believer will be filled to the limit of his capacity to "show forth the praises of him who hath called you out of darkness into His marvelous light" (1 Peter 2:9).[4]

Isn't that a marvelous picture? You and I, who have demonstrated our ability to glorify God while on earth, will be rewarded by an ability to glorify God in heaven. Throughout eternity, working and worshiping in the new heaven, the new earth, and the new Jerusalem, we will glorify God with every ounce of our strength!

Will You Be Involved in the Wedding?

If you do not know for certain that you will be part of the bride of Christ, Jesus stands willing to receive you today. Do not wait; Jesus may come to gather his bride sooner than you think. You have his invitation and promise. Wherever you are, you can lift your thoughts and voice to God and surrender your life to him.

Those who do not claim Christ's redeeming work may be like the apostle Paul, who, before coming face-to-face with Jesus on the road to Damascus, participated in just about every religious activity you could name. He knew a lot about doing good works. He had been super-religious practically from birth, circumcised according to religious tradition, a devout student of the law, zealous enough to persecute the church, and a faultless keeper of Israel's rules and religious rituals.

> But whatever was to my profit I now consider loss for the sake of Christ. What is more, I consider everything a loss compared to the surpassing greatness of knowing Christ

Jesus my Lord, for whose sake I have lost all things. I consider them rubbish, that I may gain Christ.

Philippians 3:5–8

All of the religious activities Paul participated in before his decision to follow Christ were, to use his own word, *rubbish.*

Please don't think that just because you are young, you have plenty of time to think about your eternal destiny. Life is brief and uncertain, but Jesus is inviting you to join his bride right now. "Yet to all who received him, to those who believed in his name, he gave the right to become children of God—children born not of natural descent, nor of human decision or a husband's will, but born of God" (John 1:12–13).

If you are not absolutely certain you will be part of the bride of Christ, please consider praying a prayer like this:

Lord God, King of kings, I give myself to you, trusting you for all things, thanking you for washing away my sins with the blood of your precious Son, Jesus. Fill me with your Spirit, and teach me how to live as the daughter of a king—the King of kings! Amen.

If you are a Christian, take some time today to consider what you have done to merit a crown when you stand before Christ's judgment seat. Will you wear the incorruptible crown? The crown of glory? The crown of life? The crown of rejoicing? The crown of righteousness?

What will fill your hope chest when you prepare to dress yourself in acts of righteousness? Will you stand before Christ as a glittering bride, or will your hands and face be smudged with soot from your works that disappeared in smoke and ashes?

Foreshadowing of Things to Come

We have already seen how wise Solomon believed we could possess crowns today through godly living. Other Scriptures also employ this metaphor, including Isaiah 61:10: "I delight greatly in the Lord; my soul rejoices in my God. For he has clothed me with garments of salvation and arrayed me in a robe of righteousness, as a bridegroom adorns his head like a priest, and as a bride adorns herself with her jewels."

The hymn writer William Cushing used the symbolism of jewels and crowns to describe our glorious reunion with Christ:

> When he cometh, when he cometh to make up His jewels,
> All His jewels, precious jewels, His loved and His own:
> Like the stars of the morning, His bright crown adorning,
> They shall shine in their beauty, Bright gems for His crown.
> He will gather, He will gather the gems for His kingdom,
> All the pure ones, all the bright ones, His loved and His own.
> Like the stars of the morning, His bright crown adorning,
> They shall shine in their beauty, Bright gems for His crown.

Will you be among the jewels gathered when Christ, the heavenly bridegroom, returns to collect his bride? Will you shine in his glory at that reunion?

As we move through the rest of this day and this week, may we keep our eyes focused on the end of earthly time and the beginning of our lives in Jesus' presence. By living lives of faithful, disciplined obedience now, we will be able to one day joyfully and gratefully cast our crowns at Jesus' feet. We will shine like the stars in the heavens, reflecting *his* glory!

I can't wait.

NOTES

Chapter 2: Crowns Meant for You Today

1. "Crown," *Easton's 1897 Bible Dictionary CD*.
2. Thomas Stanley and William Danko, *The Millionaire Next Door* (New York: Pocket Books, 1998).

Chapter 3: A Heavenly Contest

1. Rita Bennett, *To Heaven and Back* (Grand Rapids: Zondervan, 1997), 132.
2. J. Dwight Pentecost, *Things to Come* (Grand Rapids: Academie Books, 1958), 221.
3. Ibid., 223.
4. H. L. Willmington, *The King is Coming* (Wheaton, IL: Tyndale, 1988), 38.
5. Oswald Chambers, *My Utmost Devotional Bible* (Nashville: Nelson, 1992), 147.
6. Quoted in Joni Eareckson Tada, *Heaven: Your Real Home* (Grand Rapids: Zondervan, 1995), 195.

Chapter 4: The Crown of Thorns

1. H. L. Willmington, *The King is Coming* (Wheaton, IL: Tyndale, 1988), 34–35.
2. Athol Dickson, personal correspondence with Angela Hunt, 16 August 2002, and 11 April 2003.
3. Ibid.
4. Oswald Chambers, *My Utmost Devotional Bible* (Nashville: Nelson, 1992), 44.

Chapter 5: The Incorruptible Crown

1. John Ortberg, *The Life You've Always Wanted* (Grand Rapids: Zondervan, 1997), 50.
2. Quoted in Angela Elwell Hunt, "Spiritual Disciplines," *Evangel*, 20 March 1994, 4–5.
3. Jan Winebrenner, *Intimate Faith: A Woman's Guide to the Spiritual Disciplines* (New York: Warner, 2003), 32.
4. Rita Bennett, *To Heaven and Back* (Grand Rapids: Zondervan, 1997), 137.

5. Quoted in Angela Elwell Hunt, "Spiritual Disciplines," *Evangel*, 20 March 1994, 4–5.

6. Ibid.

7. Ibid.

8. Catherine Marshall, *A Closer Walk* (Grand Rapids: Chosen Books, 1986), 102–4.

9. For more information on spiritual disciplines, read I*ntimate Faith: A Woman's Guide to the Spiritual Disciplines* by Jan Winebrenner, *The Spirit of the Disciplines: Understanding how God Changes Lives* by Dallas Willard, *Celebration of Discipline: The Path to Spiritual Growth by Richard Foster*, or *The Life You've Always Wanted* by John Ortberg.

Chapter 6: The Crown of Rejoicing

1. Bruce and Becky Durost Fish, *George Whitefield* (Uhrichsville, OH: Barbour, 2000), 9.

2. Ibid.

3. J. C. Ryle, Select Sermons of *George Whitefield* (Carlisle, PA: The Banner of Truth Trust, 1997), 31.

4. Bernard Ruffin, *Fanny Crosby* (New York: Pilgrim Press, United Church Press, 1976), 136.

5. Dr. Clyde Narramore, personal interview with Angela Hunt, 28 April 1986, Lynchburg, Virginia.

Chapter 7: The Crown of Life

1. William Tyndale website, "Fire for the Ploughman," http://www.william tyndale.com.

2. Ibid.

3. William Tyndale website, "William Tyndale: Bible Translator, Reformer, and Martyr," http://www.williamtyndale.com.

4. George Gedda, "State Department: Chinese Leaders May Perceive Threat," Associated Press, http://www.sltrib.com/202/oct/10082002/nation_w/5160.htm.

5. William Tyndale website, "William Tyndale: Bible Translator, Reformer, and Martyr," http://www.williamtyndale.com.

6. Rita Bennett, To Heaven and Back (Grand Rapids: Zondervan, 1997), 141.

7. Ruth Tucker, *Sacred Stories: Daily Devotions from the Family of God* (Grand Rapids: Zondervan, 1989), 220, citing Della Olson, A Woman of Her Times (Minneapolis: Free Church Press, 1977), 53–54.

8. Evelyn Bence, *Spiritual Moments with the Great Hymns* (Grand Rapids: Zondervan, 1997), 136.

Chapter 8: The Crown of Glory

1. Angela Elwell Hunt, "Amy Carmichael: Let the Little Children Come," *Fundamentalist Journal*, 28 May 1986.
2. Nancy Robbins, *God's Madcap: The Story of Amy Carmichael* (Fort Washington, PA: The Christian Literature Crusade, 1974), 67.
3. Ibid., 68.
4. Mission Frontiers website, "A Living Legacy," http://www.missionfrontiers.org/1999/08/amycarm.html.
5. H. L. Willmington, *The King is Coming* (Wheaton, IL: Tyndale, 1988), 32.
6. Christopher M. Peters, "Focus on Leadership: Truett Cathy," http://www.pka.com/wcathy.html.

Chapter 9: The Crown of Righteousness

1. Jean Fleming, *The Homesick Heart*, cited in "Glimpses of Glory," *Discipleship Journal*, July–August 2003, 57.
2. Joni Eareckson Tada, *Heaven ... Your Real Home* (Grand Rapids: Zondervan, 1995), 110.
3. Lyle Hillegas, quoted in Russell Chandler, *Doomsday: The End of the World, A View Through Time* (Ann Arbor, MI: Servant, 1993), 208.

Chapter 10: The Lamb's Beautiful Bride

1. "O Bride of Christ, Rejoice" found in a 1632 Danish hymnal. The English translator is unknown.
2. H. L. Willmington, *The King is Coming* (Wheaton, IL: Tyndale, 1988), 31.
3. Randy Alcorn, *The Treasure Principle* (Sisters, OR: Multnomah, 2001), 39.
4. John Hagee, *From Daniel to Doomsday* (Nashville: Nelson, 1999), 119.
5. Ibid., 121.
6. J. Vernon McGee, *Revelation, Chapters 14–22* (Nashville: Nelson, 1991), 128.
7. Dennis Jernigan, *A Mystery of Majesty* (Monroe, LA: Howard, 1997), 85.

Chapter 11: Crown Him with Many Crowns!

1. Rita Bennett, *To Heaven and Back* (Grand Rapids: Zondervan, 1997), 171.
2. John Hagee, *From Daniel to Doomsday* (Nashville: Nelson, 1999), 123.
3. J. Vernon McGee, *Revelation: Chapters 1–5* (Nashville: Nelson, 1991), 137.
4. J. Dwight Pentecost, *Things to Come* (Grand Rapids: Academie Books, 1958), 225–26.